CHEATERS & BROKEN HEARTS
SURVIVING THE LOVE TRIANGLE

Kitten K. Jackson

♥

DISCLAIMER

In choosing to read the contents of this book, you acknowledge that you are aware of the fact that the author is NOT a therapist, a psychiatrist, or an attorney. You understand that the content of this book is NOT professional advice. The information contained herein is based upon the opinions of the author with regard to the experiences of others, as well as her own, and should be used for entertainment purposes only.

Dedication

This book is dedicated to my mom, Betty Pace Jackson, without whom I don't know how I could've made it through life so far. She's always had my back, no matter what craziness and heartache came my way. Thank you, Mom. I love you. And to my little Peej: I love you and miss you, precious.

Praise for
Cheaters & Broken Hearts

"Kitten Jackson approaches the topic of infidelity with respect, openness, and humility. Using her own experiences, and those that have been shared with her, she creates a place where anyone who has been touched by this can relate in a real way. I would recommend this book to anyone who is suffering due to infidelity."

--Elaine Barris, author of *Master For Tonight* & *Master For Tonight II*

"Kitten Jackson's *Cheaters & Broken Hearts* website and book have done more for my healing than any of the other resources I have come across. It is practical help, written with the compassion of someone who has gone through it, to guide you through those darkest hours. Her understanding of where you are and her ability to teach you how to deal with it are invaluable."

--Charlotte Forkum

"I first started following Kitten's writing on the *Cheaters & Broken Hearts* website, and I also enjoy her works of fiction. *C&BH* would be helpful for anyone who is in a painful relationship that involves infidelity. I found it to be well written, informative, easy to read, and really honest. It's a must read if you've ever been in a love triangle."

--Vickie Tullius Thall

Contents

Acknowledgments

I would like to thank the hundreds of thousands of amazing visitors to the *Cheaters & Broken Hearts* website, who reinforced my conviction that this book should be written. I'm sorry that I can't speak with each of you individually—I wish I could. I hope that you find the additional information in this book helpful.

Thanks to my awesome Facebook friends who gave me their insight, stories, and suggestions for certain parts of the book. You guys are great! Thank you, Stacy Barraza, Sheila Colston, Charlotte Forkum, Cara Correll, Denise Bond, Mark Jones P.I., and all the others for your contributions!

Thanks to my husband and family for loving me and putting up with my insatiable drive to write.

To my Peejie Peej: Thank you for being my best friend in the world! I love you and miss you more than you could ever imagine. I wrote many of these words with you right by my side, as always. Your love and patience are priceless. You are my shadow, and I still feel you with me all the time. I look forward to seeing you again someday, holding your precious body, kissing your sweet, furry little face, and looking into those beautiful brown eyes. We'll have lots of treats! Until I see you again… Mommy loves you, sweet girl!

To the men who caused me so much agony, by either cheating on me or getting involved with me while you were with someone else: I forgive you. What you did will never be okay, but I don't want to cause you any pain. I've learned from my mistakes with you, and those experiences have given me the opportunity to help others. God can make lemonade out of lemons—thanks for being my lemons.

Introduction

First, I'd like to welcome you and thank you for making ***Cheaters & Broken Hearts*** a part of your journey toward healing. It's certainly not an easy trip, but whether you believe it or not, you will get through this. You'll not only survive it, but you'll thrive!

I don't have to tell you that being involved in a love triangle, regardless of which side you're on, is a terribly painful experience. Since you're reading this book, I'm sure you already know that. Let's face it—love hurts, especially when a third person is involved. You probably also know that infidelity not only causes you to question the validity of your relationship, but it also makes you doubt your own judgment.

You wonder how you could've trusted, not to mention loved, someone who could make the conscious decision to hurt you so deeply. If you made the mistake of believing he was trustworthy, you have to wonder why you should trust *yourself* at all. If you're cheating, you're asking yourself what that says about your relationship with your partner. If you're the other woman, you're probably wondering why you're allowing yourself to be treated like a toy.

As the betrayed partner, you question what you did or didn't do, what you are or are not, that might've caused your partner to be unfaithful. You want to feel like you have some control, so you try to figure out

1

how you could've prevented it and how you can stop it. But the simple truth is that in most cases, you couldn't have prevented it, no matter what you did or didn't do, because it had nothing to do with you. There are definitely exceptions, but most of the time, it's a matter of chemistry and opportunity.

There are many factors that affect a person's strengths, weaknesses, successes, failures, and choices—everything from our relationships with our parents, to our DNA. All those factors also affect our relationships as adults, as well as the choices we make.

In order to for you to heal from the damage caused by infidelity, you have to learn to forgive, and the key to forgiveness is acceptance and understanding. In this book, I'll share the different points of view, giving you some insight. Hopefully, in learning about the different sides of the love triangle, you can get on with your healing, which will be good for you and your relationships, current and future.

Hey, don't roll your eyes! I know you don't want to forgive, and you couldn't care less about their points of view. You only care about your own feelings right now, and you want to know how to get through this nightmare. But you need to trust me on this. As long as you think that way, you're going to have a seriously tough row to hoe. (In case you're wondering, that's southern for 'a difficult task to carry out.')

Look at it this way: You're already angry and full of resentment, hate, and unforgiveness. How's that working for you? Not well at all, I would imagine. It never worked for me. What would it hurt to try it my way? You're pretty miserable, so what do you have to lose?

Remember, this is not magic. It's not a silver bullet. But if you'll read all of this book with an open mind and do what I suggest, you'll not only get through this, but you'll feel much better about yourself, and in general. If you only read the parts you think apply to you specifically, you'll miss the whole purpose of the book... and your opportunity to heal.

As strange as it might seem, you'll see a day when you'll look back on this and laugh. Okay, you might not laugh, but you won't cry, either. I'm living proof of that. There have been many times when I wanted to crawl into a hole and die because of some of the same things you're experiencing. But I did what I had to do, and I'm okay now. And you will be, too. That's not to say we might not go through the whole thing again someday, God forbid! You never know. But if we do, we'll survive that, too!

If you've read all the articles on the **C&BH** website, you'll recognize some parts of this book, but almost half of it is new. In the sections that are on the site, I've changed some things around and added more information, so please read all of it.

Why Should I Trust You?

Why should you trust me? Because I've been there. I know you feel alone. You feel like no one understands, but I do. Most people who have been involved in love triangles have only seen this puppy from one point of view. Maybe two. But I've been on all sides of the blasted thing, and they all suck!

Please don't misunderstand me. I'm not proud of any of it. In fact, I'm really embarrassed about it. I hung my head in shame for many years, but I always knew that it was a very common problem. A huge percentage of people I talked to had been on one or more sides of the triangle, and most of them were dealing with pain and shame because of it.

Eventually, I realized that maybe these things had happened to me for a reason (aside from bad choices). I'm a writer. It's what I do. Maybe I had been through all that agony so I could write about it and help someone else. That's when I decided to create my **Cheaters & Broken Hearts** website.

I answered lots of emails from desperate people looking for personalized help in the beginning. I enjoyed doing that, but it became overwhelming. There were just too many requests, and I didn't have the time to respond anymore. That's when I knew I had to do more. I had to write this book.

I'm sure I'll be accused of capitalizing on the pain *I've* caused by believing the lies of the men I've been with. I was accused of that when I published my first novel, *Keeping Secrets*, because some woman assumed it was an autobiographical cheating story. *Keeping Secrets* is fiction, and it's not even about infidelity—it's about murder.

Cheaters & Broken Hearts is not about money. As of the time of publication of this book, the website has never been monetized, so not only has it not made me any money, but it's cost me money since I published it in May of 2011. I've paid over $21 a month for four years to have the site up, in hopes that it could help someone—that's about $1,000! Yikes! And it's helped lots of people. They've told me in private messages, and that warms my heart. It reinforces my belief that things happen for a reason. I know they do. And I know I went through all that heartache, so I could help others.

That's what ***Cheaters & Broken Hearts*** is about—trying to help people with the things I've learned. It's an attempt to make amends for my mistakes and to give hope to others who might be going through something similar. And it's me, trying to make lemonade out of my lemons.

Okay, you're probably thinking something like, *You said you had been on all sides of the love triangle, but what does that mean?* I have to be careful. I can't reveal information that would be specific enough for people to be identified. The last thing I want to do is cause more pain. But I will give you some glimpses into my horror.

So… my first real experience in a triangle was when I was a teen. A married man had an affair with me for about 7 months when I was in 11th grade. That was more about an adult taking advantage of a vulnerable child, but in my mind, I was grown. I saw us as two consenting adults in a relationship. Even though I was mature for my age, nothing could've prepared me for the emotional damage visited upon me during and afterward.

Being the other woman is painful enough for an adult, but for a girl, it was devastating. I contemplated suicide daily for several years and cried for him for almost ten years. It changed me forever; the scars still linger. He taught me that was what relationships and marriage were like and that men were not to be trusted, which set the stage for what was to come.

Later, I was in the first of two physically violent relationships. After years of abuse, I knew I had to get out in order to survive. To muster the courage to leave, I got involved briefly with a couple of guys. I felt bad about being unfaithful, even though my husband had cheated on me during the whole time we were together. He always denied it, but it was obvious. He wasn't good at hiding the evidence. I was never sure who they were, but there was no doubt that he was doing it. Anyway, I wish things hadn't happened the way they did, but that was what it took for me to get out of a dangerous situation, so I can't regret those encounters completely.

I could go on, but I won't. Like the old saying, *I was looking for love in all the wrong places.* But I'm not fishing for sympathy here. Just stating facts. And there were other men who cheated on me—several. Probably even more than I'm aware of. Maybe even now. Who knows?

Some of you are probably thinking I deserved my pain for being the 'other woman.' I understand, but I hope that your anger toward anyone who might've made the mistake of falling for another woman's man won't keep you from reading this book, which could help you achieve the healing you so desperately need. And you can be sure that I've suffered beyond anything you would ever suspect. I honestly can't decide which is more painful—being the other woman or the betrayed. I'm sure you think you know, but until you've experienced both sides, you don't.

I use the term *betrayed* to describe the person whose partner has cheated on her. But the truth is that the other woman is also betrayed, because not only is she lied to, manipulated, and used, but the man she loves goes home to another woman every night. So she also feels as if she's being cheated on. And really, she is. He builds a relationship with her, making promises, telling her he loves her, that he wants to marry her, that he's leaving his wife, and so on. She loves him, so she believes him. Meanwhile, his wife is his legitimate woman, and the other woman is nothing to him in the eyes of the rest of the world—she doesn't exist.

I remember back in high school, when I was with the married guy, thinking that there seemed to be two kinds of women. One kind was the sort of 'average mom type,' whom men wanted to marry. The other was the 'sex kitten,' with whom men wanted to… well, have sex. (No, that's not where I got my name. And no, I was never a stripper. My dad named me *Kitten* as a baby.)

5

I never saw a woman who seemed to embody both of those types. I remember saying, "I want to be a mom, but I don't want to look like a mom." I wanted to be desired, but I had no idea how that choice would affect me. I didn't understand what that choice meant. There was no way for me to know I had chosen a road that would hurt me so much that I would have suicidal tendencies for many years of my life.

So here's the bottom line: Would you rather listen to someone who can speak from experience, or someone with a degree but hasn't 'been there'? Since I'm not a licensed therapist, I'm not locked into that same psychobabble you'd get from all the psychologists, therapists, and psychiatrists whose books are basically the same.

Don't get me wrong. I'm all for therapy, which you'll see in this book. And I've studied psychology independently for years. But I've had some bad experiences with therapists who appeared to be judging me, throwing words at me, but obviously having no personal knowledge of what it was like to be in the screwed-up situations I found myself in. They didn't truly understand my pain. (If you've tried therapy, and your therapist was like that, find a new one. They aren't all like that.)

Given the choice, I'd much rather listen to someone who's not so far above it—someone who's experienced these things and knows how much it hurts. Wouldn't you?

Chapter 1

What *Is* Cheating?

That's probably a matter of opinion to some degree. However, unless you're extremely liberal and like an open relationship, I'm pretty sure we'd agree on most points.

I think it's safe to say that we all see intercourse with someone outside your marriage or committed relationship as cheating. We expect monogamy under those circumstances. Even the cheater can agree with that, unless he's delusional. Don't get me started!

But what about oral sex? What about a 'handie' (hand job)? Kissing? Holding hands? Phone sex? I don't know about you, but in my opinion, they're all cheating.

What about those online connections? There are many names for it— cybersex, internet affairs, virtual relationships.... They are basically emotional relationships that do not involve physical contact. That is, at first. Many affairs that begin as strictly emotional relationships quickly turn physical.

A lot of people begin online affairs with others who are also married and live many miles away, intentionally creating a physical distance between them that would be extremely difficult to travel. They think that type of relationship is safe, since it would prevent them from physically being together, even if they were both willing to take that step. However, the longer it goes on, the more likely they will be to make that trip.

People who are involved in emotional relationships defend their actions, insisting that they are 'innocent,' because there hasn't been any physical contact. But can they honestly say that they've never discussed sex? That's not to mention participating in phone sex, graphic sexual emails, or 'sexting' (sending graphic photos or comments via text message).

Just as Bill Clinton once tried to redefine what constitutes sex, in order to save his own unfaithful butt by saying that fellatio didn't count as sex, the emotional versus physical affair debate is an attempt to redefine cheating. The 'innocent' cheaters want their partners to accept the idea that sharing their thoughts and feelings to the point that they fall in love is not cheating unless there is physical/sexual contact. I'll guarantee you this: If the shoe were on the other foot, they'd have a different view of the matter. There would be no question as to whether or not an emotional affair was cheating.

On his TV show, I heard Dr. Drew Pinsky say that men normally cheat for sexual reasons, and many times, their indiscretions involve drugs and/or alcohol. No surprise there. He also said that women usually cheat for emotional reasons, because of a lack of emotional intimacy in their relationships. I don't think this is a shock to anyone, but it confirms what I believe. Women need to feel loved, and if their partners don't meet that need, women are tempted to become involved with someone who will fulfill them in that way. For women, the sex is usually secondary to love, just as it is in any romantic relationship.

So we know why women get involved in emotional, nonphysical relationships, which is fairly obvious. But since they aren't actually having sex, why do *men* participate in them? I have a theory. Just as in the physical infidelity, they become engrossed in mental and emotional cheating because they are bored. I believe that men also need to feel as if they are wanted, if not loved, and the intense romantic excitement of a new woman is like a drug to them. That rush of endorphins literally feels like a drug-induced high. And the attention they get from the new woman feeds their self-esteem and makes them feel more alive—more like a man. Even if they know the

8

affair won't become physical, the writing and talking about sex arouses them and gives them something to fantasize about and maybe something to hope for.

I've often thought about the differences in relationships. Some are based on sex, and others are much more emotionally intimate. I don't know how you feel, but if I had a choice, I'd rather my husband have a random, disconnected sexual one-nighter with a stranger than a deep, emotionally intimate love affair that was never consummated. I hope I don't ever have to deal with that sort of thing again, but you never know… until you know.

It's easy to get caught up in a nonphysical relationship. It can start out as a friendship, completely innocent, and turn romantic and then sexual. You have to be careful when communicating with anyone with whom you feel any type of attraction. If you find yourself thinking of that person more than you would anyone else, back off. Guard your heart, especially with regard to anyone you ever dated or with whom you've ever been intimate on any level.

If you're involved in a nonphysical, emotional relationship, and you don't consider it cheating, think about this: How would you feel if your partner were doing exactly the same thing you're doing? Would you be okay with it? Would you feel betrayed? Would it hurt you? Would you continue to trust your partner? Would you see it as cheating?

And if you find that your partner has been involved in that type of relationship, don't buy into the nonsense about it being 'innocent' because it wasn't physical. And really, when he's thinking of her while he's with you, or while he's masturbating, is that not physical? In his mind, he's with her, and he's reaching orgasm while thinking of being with her, so it's definitely not innocent.

Cheating is not dependent upon "what the definition of 'is' is." It's just as much about what's going on in your heart and mind as it is about what's going on in your pants. Just remember that the next time you pick up your cell phone to send that sexy text or flirty email. Chances are very good that your partner would think of it as cheating, whether the person on the receiving end of those texts or emails had ever been physically intimate with you or not. Is it worth breaking the heart of the one you love? If not, don't do it.

Why Did He Cheat?

Okay, I have to say it, even though I know it won't do any good. Don't let yourself go there! But you will. It's inevitable. You want to try to figure out what went wrong, so you can hopefully stop it from happening again. Trust me—even if you knew there were things you did wrong, and you fixed every one of them, there's no guarantee it wouldn't happen again. Sorry.

First, please understand that I'm *not* saying it's your fault that he cheated on you! It wasn't. And I'm *not* saying that he was justified in doing it, either! He wasn't. What I am saying is that people tend to try to justify their actions by pointing out their partners' flaws or negative traits. For example, how many times have you heard men say something like, "She just let herself go," or, "She's gained so much weight that I'm not attracted to her anymore"? Or maybe you've heard women say, "All he cares about is the TV," or, "He never listens to me."

Even if you were perfect in every way, the ones I call *serial cheaters* would say, "She's just too perfect. She makes me feel inadequate." The serial cheaters are unfaithful, no matter whom they are with or what the circumstances. If you're with a guy like that, don't worry about how you could improve yourself or the relationship. It wouldn't matter.

However, if your partner is a good, decent person whom you believe is actually regretful about his infidelity, and if you believe you could forgive and trust him again, it might not be a lost cause. But I strongly urge you to get couples counseling *before* you recommit to the relationship. Do not think that therapy is a magic pill, though. Some couples can work through instances of infidelity, and others can't.

It takes a really strong, secure person to be able to give a cheater another chance. If you choose to do that, make sure that God is a part of your relationship. Though having Him involved won't make your marriage affair-proof, without Him, you're fighting a losing battle.

Regardless of whether or not you continue the relationship, it's always best to take a good, long look at it. Obviously, he cheated, which always involves deception, if not blatant lies. But what else is wrong between you? I suggest that you make two 'pros and cons' lists—one about your partner and one about the relationship.

Then ask yourself the following questions:

* Do I love him?

* Does he love me?

* Was I happy with him before he cheated?

* Was he happy with me before he cheated?

* Have we been emotionally, as well as physically, intimate in recent months?

* How often do we have sex?

* When we have sex, is it more like making love, or is it hurried and selfish?

* Does he care about my feelings?

* Do I care about his feelings?

* How well do we get along?

* Do we want the same things in life (same goals)?

* Have we grown apart?

* Is he committed to our relationship?

* Am I committed to our relationship?

* Why are we together (love, good sex, children, money)?

* Do we respect each other?

* Do we like each other?

* Do we enjoy being together (have fun together)?

* Do we allow each other freedom to be ourselves?

* When we disagree, are we civil, or are we abusive?

* Do we get violent?

* How did we get to this point?

* What is his part in getting here?

* What is my part in getting here?

* Why do I want to stay with him?

* Why does he want to stay with me?

* Do I want him because someone else does, and I can't stand to lose?

* Do I want him because I love him?

Now it's time to take a look at yourself. Even the best of us contribute in some ways when we are in a crippled or dying relationship. We feel hurt, so we lash out. Or maybe we take the passive-aggressive route and 'forget' to pick up his dry cleaning, or we 'forget' to move the wet towel off his side of the bed.

Most of the time, men who cheat say that it's because of the way the new lovers make them feel. That's not just about chemistry and sexual technique. It's also about the way she makes him feel *about himself*, too. We might not be able to change the chemistry we have with someone, but there are other aspects of the relationship over which we do have some control.

As previously mentioned, cheaters like to try to justify their actions by pointing out the shortcomings of their partners. Sometimes those are just words—lame excuses for what they don't want to take responsibility for. But sometimes, there is validity in those words. Again, I'm not blaming the victim or condoning infidelity! I'm just saying that it is what it is.

Here's an example: A man wants to have sex with his wife. She 'allows it' maybe once or twice a month but only with lots of restrictions. No oral, no kissing, no talking dirty, no touching of undesignated areas, etc. He feels undesirable and inadequate. He doesn't believe his wife loves him anymore. Then on a business trip, he meets an attractive woman who seems to be interested in him. They talk, share a dinner and drinks, and then she touches his leg. Sparks fly. She begins to fill the void in him that his wife has no interest in filling. They kiss, and he's toast! Not okay, and certainly not right, but it's not difficult to see how and why he would be vulnerable.

And here's a real-life example: I have several friends who are writers. One of them, Sarah, became so engrossed in the writing and promotion of her books that when her husband was at home, she had no time for him at all. They still slept together, but that was about it. He tried to tell her she was ignoring him and that he missed her, but she couldn't stop chasing her dream long enough to spend any quality time with him.

Then Sarah noticed that her husband seemed to be distracted and not so interested in being with her. She started doing a little investigative work and found that he was seeing another woman. She was upset, but she said that it was partially her fault. She decided to stay with him, because, as she said, she knew she had been neglecting him and that he never would've done that if she had been giving him the attention he needed.

Because a cheater usually justifies his actions by pointing out the misdeeds of his partner, he's generally glad when the partner does something 'wrong,' so he has an excuse for his cheating. It's like a *get out of jail free* card. "It's your fault! If you hadn't…" That kind of thing. I find that infuriating, but at the same time, as Sarah admitted, there was a bit of validity. In his eyes, she wasn't the same woman he married, because she was spending all her free time on her books. If we want our men to be faithful, we have to do what we can to help them resist temptation, which means spending time with them and attempting to satisfy them sexually.

Sarah didn't do what I think I would've done. However, if I had been in that situation, and I had been talking with another man (as she was), I might feel differently. I understand her point. She wasn't without fault, so it made sense that she would be able to forgive him for his infidelity, especially since he is a good man, they've been together for many years, and he's good to her in all the ways that really matter to her.

We all have needs, and some of them are very basic, like love and security. Some of us—usually men—have stronger sex drives, while others—almost always women—have a much deeper need for emotional intimacy.

When we enter into a committed relationship, especially a marriage, we're making a commitment to at least attempt to meet the needs of our partners. If those needs are not met, your partner becomes more vulnerable to temptation.

Humans are weak, especially with regard to sex, which makes it difficult to resist. When we have loving, affectionate, considerate partners who meet our needs, we are much stronger when faced with the opportunity to stray. Perhaps it's because we can't justify cheating on someone like that. If, however, we feel neglected and unappreciated, we are much more prone to unfaithfulness.

I also understand that sometimes it's difficult to give everything he needs because of issues in the relationship, including his lies and infidelity. When you feel hurt and angry, the last thing you want to do is have sex with the man who hurt you. If that's the case, it's time to bring in a third party, a therapist, for couples counseling. If you can work through those issues, maybe you can get back to a state of mind that would allow you to feel better about giving him the attention he needs.

The moral of this story is that though there is no magic pill, being an affectionate, attentive, and considerate lover and friend to your partner is the best defense against infidelity.

Can I Prevent His Cheating?

As I've said, there is no guarantee that the one you love won't cheat. Some say that given the perfect set of circumstances, anyone could succumb to temptation. I wish I could sell you some 'faithful dust,' so you wouldn't have any cause for concern. Unfortunately, my formula is still lacking. So it's up to us to do whatever we can to keep our partners interested, which is key.

First things first. What is the basic reason we want to have sex with a particular person? Sexual attraction! And what almost always causes the attraction initially? Physical appearance!

So we know we can't make everyone else in the world ugly, but we can do something about our own looks. I know, that's superficial.... Do you want me to blow smoke, or do you want the truth? I'm a truth girl, so here it is. When it comes to sex appeal, things like intelligence, moral character, and a good family are completely irrelevant. Maybe they should matter, but they don't. We have to face the facts.

There are some things we can't change, such as genetics. If you're short, you can't make yourself tall. Well, you could wear heels, but that's another chapter. However, there are ways in which we can make the most of what we have. Most of it is simple logic.

As we all know, in order to look our best, we have to eat a healthy diet, drink plenty of water, get eight hours of sleep each night, and get adequate exercise. I mean, be honest. How hot would you be for a guy who had gained 100 pounds since your wedding and got winded just walking to the kitchen to get another bowl of ice cream?

Granted, doing that healthy stuff is not easy. I know I don't do all that. I want to. I intend to. But somehow, I get derailed, usually by my husband, who thinks that pizza is one of the major food groups, and dessert is another. New Year's resolution: Get in better shape and wean myself off of carbs!

Some more basic suggestions are to shower and shave! It might sound silly, but many people neglect their hygiene unless they're going out.

And think about what you wear. Sweat pants and ponytails are okay sometimes. They're comfortable, but they aren't sexy to most guys, especially if it's your everyday attire. Some nice jeans and a pretty top, or maybe a sundress, would be a nice surprise for your guy. Doing your hair and adding a little makeup, cologne, and nail polish also makes a difference.

The more you do to make yourself attractive to your partner, the more he will appreciate you, and the less vulnerable he will be when, not if, he's faced with temptation. Feeling unsatisfied, unappreciated, and unloved makes us weaker, so anything we can do to prevent our partners from feeling that way should work in our favor.

This is a good one. Think of what would make you feel good. I'm sure you can think of something your partner would enjoy. How about a nice home-cooked meal for him? Or a massage? You get the idea.

How long has it been since you and your partner sat together and held hands? What about taking a shower or bath together? It's important that you reconnect (or stay connected) with your partner. Write a note, a letter, or maybe a poem telling your partner how special he is. Write a sexy note on the bathroom mirror with your lipstick, a bar of soap, or a Sharpie. Affection is essential, and it can't be overemphasized.

Now, for the most obvious thing—sex! Get a sitter for the kids and have some fun with your partner! It's up to each of us to keep it from getting boring. Instead of pushing the buttons in the usual order, mix it up. Linger where you normally don't even go. Try something new. You know what your partner likes—do it! The more you do for him, the more he'll want to do for you, and the less he'll be able to justify even pondering the idea of cheating.

I don't think any of this is big news, but sometimes it takes having the obvious pointed out to make us focus on things we do every day without thinking. The things we do affect those around us, so we need to think about those effects and try to do what we can to make ourselves and our homes more appealing to our partners. It might just make them want to come home, rather than going out "with the guys."

The Importance of Sex

Forgive my redundancy. I know I've mentioned several times that sex is important, but I have to! I don't think there are many men out there who don't understand how critical it is in a relationship, but there are lots of women who just do not get it. They seem to have the attitude that since they 'got him,' they don't have to work to keep him. If only it were that easy.

We have to remember that men are almost perpetually in a state of arousal. It takes nothing more than a look, a word, or just waking up in the morning, and they're ready for action. If you don't take care of your man's sexual needs, don't be surprised if he finds someone who will. That's not to say that infidelity is acceptable! It's not! But when you look at the reality of the situation, you'll see that it's not only possible—it's likely. And the better looking he is and the more money he has, the more women will find him attractive, and the harder it'll be for him to battle against his testosterone, which is a terribly strong motivator.

There are some cases of infidelity that begin with an emotional attachment to someone, but most of the time, it's about chemistry—sexual attraction. And as I said before, it almost always begins with what we see. It's exciting, it's fun, and it makes you feel young. It's like a drug, and it's difficult to resist, even when you have a good sex life at home. But to someone who is feeling sexually frustrated, an opportunity to have sex is like a newly sober alcoholic getting a bottle of Crown Royal for his birthday. He might not have the strength to say 'no.'

Maybe you're thinking, *I take care of my responsibilities. I let him do me.* Think again! How would you feel if you were the one who wanted him, and he *allowed* you to have sex with him because it was required? He wants you to not only participate, but also to enjoy it. He wants you to want him. And most men would love to have their wives initiate sex occasionally, if not more.

After couples have spent a few years together, they begin to get a little (or a lot) lazy in bed. They know how to get their partners to orgasm, so they get in a rut of doing exactly the same things, in exactly the same order. No talking, and sometimes, not even kissing. Very little foreplay, if any. Well, that might get the job done, but is it exciting? Is it something he's going to be thinking about while he's at work tomorrow, and his sexy assistant is flirting with him? Probably not.

Think of the past fireworks.

So you don't find him as attractive as you used to. He might feel the same about you, but if you love him, and you want to hold onto him and not lose him to someone who does find him attractive, you need to start thinking of him differently. Think of the way you felt about him when you first met. Think of the sparks, the fireworks, the animal attraction…. It was awesome, wasn't it? What happened? Bills, children, careers, housework, weight gain? I know. Things change, and things get in the way. But that doesn't mean you can't still have that spark. Talk to him. Then start doing something about it.

Get dolled up.

One of the easiest things you can do to spice up things in bed is to wear some sexy panties, a teddy, or a pretty baby doll. And don't forget the high-heeled sandals! But make sure to paint your toenails. ~Wink~ Even guys without foot fetishes like to see pretty feet.

So you don't look like you did when you married him, and you're embarrassed to wear lingerie. I feel that way, too. But believe me, he won't mind! My hubby LOVES it! If you'll try it, you'll see I'm right. It'll mean more to him than you can imagine.

Share your fantasies

Many women have secret sex lives in the deep, dark places in their minds. They have active fantasy lives of which their husbands are not aware. They read romance novels, living vicariously through the characters in their stories. But why should those fictitious characters have all the fun? I understand—it takes a lot of trust to open up yourself and share your fantasies with your man. But if you love him, and he loves you, he would probably be thrilled to hear about your fantasies, and he might share some of his own. Sharing your fantasies together could bring a whole new intimacy and excitement between you that you never knew could exist.

If you feel humiliated by the idea of talking about it, try telling him with the lights off. Or maybe you could write your fantasies out for him. WARNING: DO NOT share fantasies about being with someone you know, especially a past lover. That would be sure to cause distrust and cause pain to your partner. If you're talking with your partner about this, give him the same warning. Things like that are without doubt better left unsaid.

Try some role playing.

After you've shared some of your fantasies, maybe you could do some role playing. Some common fantasies that people like to play out are doctor or nurse/patient, boss/secretary, and cop/criminal. You are only limited by your imagination and your willingness to participate. Maybe you could write a scenario you'd like to play, complete with dialogue. He'd probably go into character immediately!

Read some erotica.

So maybe you aren't so creative, or maybe he's not. In that case, get some help. Read some erotic stories together. You can find anything you want online. If you don't want to read them with him, read them alone before he gets home or before you go to bed. It's a great way to get in the mood. If you like vampires, which I didn't until I read these books, try *Master For Tonight* and *Master For Tonight II* by Elaine Barris. It's an erotic vampire romance. Very steamy! Well written and well edited.

Get in the mood.

As for getting in the mood... that's another issue that a lot of women have. They just aren't interested in sex. Maybe you never had much of a sex drive, or maybe it's diminished over the years. Whatever the case, it doesn't have to be that way. Part of it is probably the way you think, or don't think, about sex. Don't allow yourself to look at it as a chore, or as something you're obligated to do. Look at it as something you're blessed to have. As a woman who has spent most of her adult life in long-distance relationships or without someone, it has always amazed me that women who had husbands who loved them and wanted them didn't appreciate them. Think of your husband as a blessing, and remember that he needs to feel your love for him sexually.

For women who have hormonal issues that affect their sex drives, there are supplements that might help. I took two of them years ago for a possible hormone imbalance, but I had to stop taking them, because my sex drive became overwhelming! But **ALWAYS CHECK WITH YOUR DOCTOR OR PHARMACIST BEFORE ADDING SUPPLEMENTS TO YOUR DIET, ESPECIALLY IF YOU'RE TAKING PRESCRIPTION MEDICATIONS OR OTHER SUPPLEMENTS**, because even 'natural' ones can have **dangerous** side effects!

Tell him what gets you going!

Hopefully, this will sound ridiculous to you, but there are actually some women who have been with the same men for years, but have never told their men what turns them on physically. They expect their men to know how to please them. They might think of their partners as lousy and/or lazy lovers, but that might not be the case at all.

We're all different. We like different things. What might drive me crazy might make you throw up! If you've never talked with your partner about the things that turn you on, or things you think would feel good, it's past time! It might be a little embarrassing, but you can do it. As with the fantasies, you can always write it out for him.

When talking to a man about what you like or don't like, choose your words carefully! Be very positive. For example, "Honey, I really like it when you…." Or "I'd love it if you would…." **NEVER** say anything like, "I hate it when you…." Or "It grosses me out when you…." Remember the fragile ego. He wants to please you, so if he feels that you're criticizing him, he'll be hurt and embarrassed and feel as if he's failed you. Think of how you'd want him to teach you, and use that as your guide.

Mix it up.

Women are notorious for having sexual hang-ups. We have a fear of the unknown, so we hesitate to try new things, and we miss out on immeasurable pleasure just because we're afraid, embarrassed, or unsure.

For clarity, I'm not suggesting that you have a ménage à trois. I think that's a mistake for any couple, and I suggest that you think long and hard before doing something like that. If your partner is pushing you to have a three-way, he's probably only a short step away from cheating, if he hasn't taken that step already. (Talking about it as in a fantasy is fine, but doing it is something else entirely.)

No, what I'm talking about are things you and your partner can do together, such as making love outside, or in front of a hotel window, or maybe on your kitchen counter. Granite would be cold, but you get the picture. Mix it up!

Try some toys.

Let's talk toys. Especially for you ladies who have a difficult time achieving orgasm, a vibrator can be your best friend. If you haven't tried them before, you can go online and check them out. There are all kinds of toys you can try. Most men are completely open to this—anything to help you enjoy sex! However, before you go busting up into your bedroom with your new friend, talk to your partner about it. There are some men who are insecure, and they might see the use of toys as an insult to their 'manhood.' Explain to him that it's not that he is lacking in any way, but you're just interested in trying some new things. That should help him relax about it.

Give him oral.

Girls, there's one thing that must be discussed here. When we're in a new relationship, we usually do it, but then we gradually do it less and less as time goes on. You know what I'm talking about—oral sex. All right, don't snarl. I know that most women aren't particularly fond of giving it, and granted, it isn't the easiest thing to do, but the importance of it cannot be stressed enough. It's also critical that you not have that *I'm-gonna-puke* look on your face. It might not be completely honest, but try to look as if you're into it. It can also be exciting for you if you focus on how much pleasure you're giving him. The more you do it, the easier it'll be. But remember—**cover your teeth with your lips!**

Be careful when getting creative with oral!

I'm sure you've heard of people using whipped cream, syrup, ice cream, and other sweet things as 'toppings' for their own sweet spots, but DON'T DO IT! DO NOT EVER put anything sweet on or near the genital area—his or yours! Doing so can cause severe vaginal and urinary tract infections! I mention his, too, because if it's on him, it could go inside you. If you want to try something like that, keep it on the upper body, and DO NOT perform oral sex until you've brushed your teeth and rinsed your mouth thoroughly! And make sure your hands are clean! Also take great care to be sure that *anything* in or near the vagina is completely clean and couldn't leave any kind of residue. And **NEVER** let him go from 'back to front' with *anything*—objects, as well as body parts, including the tongue.

You might be thinking that all this is for your man, but you'd be surprised. The way it usually works is the more you do for him, the more he'll want to do for you. That doesn't only go for sex. If your man is satisfied in the bedroom, he's much more apt to be happy outside the bedroom, too. And a happy man is more likely to paint the living room than a sexually frustrated man is. So the next time your husband seems frisky, show him what you can do. Or better yet, don't wait. Out of the blue, reach over and grab his package. A little touch can go a long way!

Chapter 2

How Do I Know He's Cheating?

How do you know he's cheating? Well, if you find a condom wrapper in your bedroom, and you and your man don't use condoms, you have your smoking gun. If you find a pair of panties you know are not yours, that's almost as good as video, unless he's a cross-dresser. But not all cheaters are that careless or stupid. Some of them are stealthy, and they take great care to cover their tracks. To catch them, you have to pay close attention but not let on that you are suspicious. If they think you're onto them, they will be even more careful not to leave any evidence.

Let him think you are completely oblivious to what he's doing. That will probably be difficult, because you have to pretend to be happy, or at least content, and act as though you trust him.

If your man knows you are suspicious, or if you've already confronted him, back off! Don't mention it at all. Then after a while, gradually warm up to him. Here's the hard part—apologize to him for being suspicious. I know, that's asking a lot, but remember that getting him to let his guard down is the first step toward finding the truth.

There are probably hundreds, if not thousands, of indications or warning signs that your partner is cheating. Obviously, I won't be able to list everything, but I can give you a good sampling of them. You'll get it.

Watch out for the following clues:

Changes in sexual behavior
Does he suddenly seem different in bed? Does he have some new tricks? Maybe she's taught him a few things.

Has he recently started talking about having a three-way with a particular person? He might want to be with her without taking the risk of losing you, so he wants to include you.

Does he seem more aroused during sex than usual? Maybe he's fantasizing about someone else.

Talking about a female 'friend'
Has he been talking a lot about a woman he refers to as a 'friend'? Has he been telling you how cool she is and how much you'd like her, but when you ask about meeting her, he comes up with some excuse why you can't? He could be talking about her to you because he's seeing you more as a friend, wanting to share his excitement about her with you, but he's still not ready to let you go.

Unexplained changes in mood
Has he gone from upbeat, to grouchy? He could be thinking about her and resenting the fact that he has to be with you instead.

From bummed out, to happy? He might be excited about someone new and loving life because of her.

Changes in routine
Has he begun to 'work late' more than usual, or is he going out 'with the guys' a lot lately? That one's pretty obvious.

Changes in hygiene
Has he suddenly shaved facial hair he's had for years? Has he grown facial hair he's never had before? Has he changed his hair style? Is he shaving in places he didn't shave before? Has he changed cologne or aftershave? Does he wear cologne now, but he didn't before? He's trying to impress someone, and it might not be you.

Attention to fitness

Is he suddenly trying to tone up or lose weight? No-brainer.

Attention to style

Has he bought new clothes or shoes, especially of a different type or style than he normally wears? Has he recently bought new and/or different types of underwear than he usually wears? Maybe she told him what she liked… or maybe she bought them!

Attention to details

Is his normally dirty car or truck now spotless? Are his fingernails now clean and trimmed? Is his usually junky, grungy apartment or house now presentable? Maybe someone else is visiting.

Trying to appear to be single

Are pictures of you or the two of you no longer visible in his home or office? Does his profile picture on Facebook or other social media no longer have you in it? Or even worse, has he removed photos of you and the two of you from his Facebook page? Does he say flirty things to other women in 'comments' or in his 'status'? Has he recently changed his relationship status to 'single' or 'ask'? Don't buy into his excuses. You know what these things mean.

Becoming secretive

Has he recently changed passwords on email, voicemail, credit card accounts…? Does he leave the room when receiving a call or text? Does he hang up the phone or close computer windows when you walk into the room? Does he hide his phone from you? No explanation necessary.

Becoming 'modest'

Has he started to hide his body from you, like quickly covering with a towel or clothing if you walk into the room? Does he now want the lights off when you have sex? Has he recently had unexplained scratches on the shoulders or back, or 'bug bites' in odd places? Maybe she wants to leave some evidence, so you'll see it and know about them.

Unexplained disappearances

Does he say he's going to Walmart, but he doesn't come back for hours, and the store is only ten minutes away? Does he say he's playing golf, but doesn't take his clubs? He's probably not shopping or golfing.

Pulling away

Does he seem distant? Has he stopped kissing you? Does he resist your sexual advances? Has he stopped saying, "I love you"? Have the *I love you* calls and texts suddenly stopped? He's not into you, and he might be into someone else.

Hiding you

Has he stopped (or never started) taking you around his family or friends? Has he stopped taking you out in public? Does he tell people, "*I* watched *Breaking Bad* last night," when he watched it with you? He doesn't want her to find out he was with you.

Changing habits

Has he started doing his own laundry, when you used to do it? Has the little pile of receipts on the bureau suddenly found a secret home? He could be hiding evidence.

Nightstand drawer items missing

Does the KY Liquid seem to be disappearing without activity between the two of you to explain it? Where are all the condoms? If he didn't use them with you, he used them with someone else.

Your personal items missing

Has your vibrator disappeared from his apartment? What about your shaver? Did he recently 'need to use' the drawer he designated as yours, hiding your stuff away in a bag in the closet? Either someone else has been there, or he's hoping to have her over.

Inexplicably clean

Does he come home from 'working all day' or 'hanging out with the guys' smelling like he just got out of the shower? Maybe did shower to get rid of evidence.

Lies

Does he over-explain things? Does he give you long, detailed explanations for things you didn't even ask him about? Have you caught him in lies? Does he look like a deer caught in headlights when you ask him why he wasn't where he said he was going to be? Dude's hiding something.

I think you get the idea. As I said, this list is far from being all inclusive. However, it should give you enough info to get you started on your journey toward the truth.

Protect yourself.

After considering all these things, you think he's cheating. What if he wants to have sex with you? You should protect yourself from possible exposure to STDs. If you and your man use condoms, you're probably okay. As you know, they don't protect 100 percent, but used properly, they do give good protection.

Otherwise, I would suggest that you avoid sex with him. A 'headache' might work a time or two, but then he would know something's up. You have to find another strategy.

Ladies, if you're on the pill, tell him you forgot one, so you need to use a condom for a month or so, because it might not be safe. If he's cheating, the LAST thing he'll want is for you to be pregnant! Also, antibiotics reduce the effectiveness of the pill, so you might be able to use that excuse.

If you use an IUD, tell him you're spotting, and you're afraid it might be coming out, which does happen, so you need to see your doctor before you have sex again. If you take the birth control shot, tell him you have a friend who was taking the shot and got pregnant (I have a friend that happened to), so you want to use condoms until you can see your doctor, who is booked for the next six weeks.

Or you could say that you think you might be getting a yeast infection. If necessary, use the seven-day, over-the-counter cream. It won't hurt you. After that, say you're still having symptoms, and you need to see your doctor before you have sex, and the doc is booked.

Get a notebook.

Get a notebook and find a place to hide it where it could never be found. I mean NEVER! Somewhere like under the carpet in the corner of the guest room or in a box of junk that's been stashed away in the back of a closet forever. If you want to put it in your computer, name it something like 'Menstrual Cycle' or 'Mom's medications'—something he wouldn't be interested in.

Okay, write down everything you find even remotely suspicious. The more you write, the more real it seems, and the less you'll doubt yourself when he says you're crazy, which is standard for a cheater. They usually don't even bother with, "No, I'm not cheating!"

I think that, "You're crazy!" is the standard response, because he can at least feel as if he isn't lying—he's deflecting. It sounds pathetic, because it is, but it's just one of the rationalizations people use. "Well, I never *said* I wasn't cheating! At least, I didn't lie!" Please!

Get the proof.
The next step is getting the proof, which you'll learn about in the next section. Be careful, be diligent, and be stealthy. And good luck!

Exhibiting any one, or even a few, of these signs does not necessarily mean that your partner is cheating. Sometimes people try to make improvements to themselves and their lives, especially as New Year's resolutions. For this reason, it is important that if you suspect your partner is cheating, find the evidence *before* confronting him, making any decisions about moving out or making him leave, or going to an attorney.

Getting the Evidence

So you think he's cheating. Even if you're not convinced yet, you need to find proof to know for sure. But don't say anything about it! Don't confront him, don't ask his friends or family, and above all—do not accuse him! Now is the time for you to become your own private investigator, unless you can afford to pay a professional, and get the evidence.

First and foremost... do not get caught! Easy for me to say, right? I know you're anxious, upset, angry, and myriad other feelings that could interfere with your ability to be cool. If you get caught spying, then you end up looking like the bad guy if he isn't guilty (and sometimes, even if he is). And if he is guilty, you give him the heads up that you're onto him and that even more care should be taken not to get caught, which makes getting the proof even more difficult for you.

DISCLAIMER: Before I tell you about the ways you can try to get evidence of his cheating, I have to **WARN** you. In Michigan, a man was charged with a felony for reading his cheating wife's email! The statute covers theft of intellectual property. If convicted, the man could face up to five years in prison. **Be sure to check the laws in your state before taking *ANY* of the following suggestions!**

Check his stuff.

I'd say the easiest place to start would be to check his pockets and wallet, and look through his stuff. You'd be surprised at what guys will bring home. The following is a good example of the kinds of things you might find.

One morning, my former husband left to go to Huntsville, Alabama, which was about 50 miles away, supposedly to meet with a couple to make a sale. It was a rare thing for him to ever have a sales meeting and not come home with a contract. This was before we all had cell phones, but he did have a 'car phone.' As you can imagine, there were no answers to any of the calls I made to him that day. He showed up that night, about 7:00, with no contract! He just couldn't get them to commit, he said. I didn't buy that for a second, but what could I do?

So the next morning, I was going to do some laundry. I was emptying his pockets, which he never did, and guess what I found—a receipt from the Huntsville Hilton! He did think to put it in another man's name.

When he got home that night, I showed him the receipt. Amazingly enough, he didn't know who the guy was or how that guy's receipt got into his pocket! Shocking! As you might expect, he was 'indignant' that I had the nerve to suggest that was his receipt. And they even had room service! Jerk.

Another time, I found a prescription he had for an antibiotic commonly prescribed for certain sexually transmitted infections. He said he got a doctor to give it to him "as a precaution." Yeah, right! During those years, I didn't realize that the 'infections' I kept having, with repeated trips to the doctor's office for antibiotics, were actually STDs I was contracting from him. I knew they *could be* transmitted sexually, but I didn't know they *had to be* sexually transmitted. If you've contracted trichomoniasis, for example, ask your doctor. Someone has been jumping the fence.

Check his phones.

Next, look at the phones he uses. Unless he's stupid, he'll probably delete calls from the caller ID on the landline and calls on the cell, as well as texts (or sexts). However, if you've been really cool about the whole thing, he might be overly confident that he has your complete trust and that you would never suspect a thing. I know that sounds crazy, but I actually heard a guy say that before! He said his wife would never suspect anything and would never check up on him. It turned out that he was right!

Also, if you don't see any evidence on his phones, don't assume he's being faithful. He could have another phone, one on her account!

Check his computer.

The next easiest thing is to check his computer. Check his history and look for suspicious things such as dating sites or chat rooms. Most cheaters are smart enough to set their history to 0 days, but again, they might think they have your undying trust. If you change his history setting, he might notice, which would tip him off. Don't do that.

If you know his passwords, look at his emails. They don't like to delete the naughty ones. He's not going to name an email folder 'Hot Juicy Emails,' so look in ALL the folders, even if they have benign names like 'Taxes' or 'Bills.' And don't forget to look at his photos. But don't immediately freak out if you find a girly pic. Some guys are kind of pathetic and download pictures of women from websites or from emails their guy friends send. Just because it's a sexy picture doesn't necessarily mean it's someone he's seeing. But if it's someone he knows… that's a horse of a different color!

You've probably also heard about computer monitoring software you can install on his computer that records every keystroke. I saw one you could download for only $97.00, and it claimed to be 'invisible' (undetectable).

Check his social media

Remember that lots of people use Facebook and other social media to meet members of the opposite sex. I have a family member who found her boyfriend on Twitter! They find and contact others through those sites, because they don't look suspicious. That's why you'd need to not just look at his page, but also get into his account to see his private messages. He might be smart enough to not put the incriminating stuff out in public.

Show up at his 'watering hole.'

The next time he says he's going out with 'friends,' ask where they're going to be, and say, "I might stop by," or "I (or we, meaning you and your friends) might join you for a drink." He might say, "I don't know. I'll call you when we get there." If you don't get the call, you know he doesn't want you there. If he's evasive, saying, "Oh, I'm not sure. We'll probably hit several places," ask him to call you when he gets there. Again, if that call doesn't come, he's most likely hiding something.

If he always goes to the same place, or he tells you where they'll be, just say, "Okay. Be careful," or whatever you would normally say. After he leaves, give it about an hour and then go there. Don't go in all super-sleuth, hiding behind ficus trees and such. Just walk in like anyone else and scope the place out. If you see him talking to a woman, DO NOT PANIC! Even if they look cozy, be cool! If you're out of their line of sight, watch them. Body language is everything, especially when alcohol is involved.

If he hasn't spotted you, take out your phone and TURN OFF THE FLASH! Once you're sure the flash is off, take some pictures or get some video. Then compose yourself, try to stop shaking, and as calmly as possible, walk over to them wearing a smile. Watch for a reaction in both parties. If the woman looks shocked or surprised, or especially if she looks angry, you know your partner probably didn't tell her about you. If he looks annoyed or angry that you're there, you can be pretty sure he's either cheating or trying to cheat.

And if he isn't there, where is he? He'll come up with some lame excuse. If he says he was at another bar or club, tell him you were there, but you didn't see him. Watch for his expression. He'll probably have a brief look of panic on his face. If he's a really good liar, he might be blank for a second, but then he'll come up with some other nonsense. If he's an extremely good, well-practiced liar, he'll have another story ready, just in case the first one failed. Enjoy his discomfort and then laugh. Tell him you were kidding.

You could record his calls.

(Be careful—see **warning** below.)

There are other ways to catch a cheater of which I'm sure you've heard. We all know about machines you can use to record calls on your landline. I have a friend who caught her husband cheating that way. One model I saw was $299.95, but you could add the optional truth detection/ deception software for an additional $100.00! I'll admit that I was surprised to read about that software.

WARNING: In some states, it's illegal to record a phone conversation unless both parties are aware that the conversation is being recorded. They either have to be warned that the call is being recorded when the call begins, or the recorder has to give a signal that clicks or beeps intermittently, letting them know the phone could be tapped, which defeats the whole purpose! You could do this for your own information, but if you let the cheater know you did it, **you could be prosecuted**. And whatever you recorded wouldn't be admissible in court, because it was obtained illegally.

Nothing says "gotcha" like video.

Don't forget about the 'nanny cams,' which you can set up to catch a cheating partner. 'Cheater cams' are motion-activated hidden cameras. Some even work in the dark, but be prepared to pay a pretty penny for those! (Say that one fast three times! Ha!) One model I saw listed a sale price of $499.95! Some of them look like smoke detectors or clothing hooks—pretty stealthy.

Beware of the spy software detector.

What you might not know about is the software that can detect computer monitoring software. It lets the suspected cheater know there is spy software on the computer, in which case, you're busted. At the same time, you have to remind yourself that if he has put that type of software on his computer, he has something to hide. As Dr. Phil says, "Those who have nothing to hide, hide nothing." I love that.

*Maybe try spy *hardware*.*

If you think your partner might be suspicious that you're suspicious, don't use the spy software. You can get spy hardware for the computer. It can't be detected by software that he might install to catch you snooping. One model is priced from $89.00 to $299.00.

Track him.

And we all know about the GPS trackers you can buy to put on his vehicle, which would let you know where he is. I saw one online for $369.00.

Spy on his cell.

The next product is one of which I wasn't aware. There is software you can buy to put on a cell phone that tells you everything! You can view contact lists, read text messages, view calls made and received, and view pictures. This model was listed at $138.00, but was said to be going up to $199.00 soon. I haven't heard of any laws about this one, but you'd better check before buying it.

Make a conference call.

I have a friend, Melissa, who told me about something she did to catch a guy she suspected of lying to her. They weren't in a relationship, but I wanted to tell you about it, because it's a good way to catch someone in a lie. And it's *proof* that sometimes, the 'other woman' can be your ally.

My friend met this guy the same night she met a woman named Carrie. Since he seemed to be interested in them both, the women talked and agreed not to go out with him if he asked the other out. He asked Melissa out for Tuesday night.

Melissa talked with Carrie, and they decided to make a little conference call, without telling him that Melissa was on the line. He told Carrie he *hadn't* asked Melissa out and that he wasn't interested in her—that she wasn't his type. He asked Carrie to see him Wednesday night. She told him that Tuesday night would be better for her. He told her that was fine, because he wasn't doing anything special that night. Boom!

They then hung up, and Melissa called Carrie back. While they were talking, the guy called Melissa. She added him to the call, and he told her that something had come up, and he wondered if he could see her Wednesday night instead. She told him she couldn't, because she was going to dinner with Carrie that night.

At that point, unaware that Carrie was listening, the guy started telling Melissa that Carrie had been calling him and practically stalking him. That's when Carrie started screaming at him! Ha! Melissa told him they had both been listening to his crap and that she was not interested in dating him... ever. Carrie told him the same. He hung up, but then he had the nerve to call them both back! Players....

Check his undies!

Get ready, people, because I saved the best for last. I was shocked at this one. Are you sitting down? It's a semen detector! It was marketed for women to find semen in a man's underwear, but how much more damning and convicting would it be to find semen in a woman's panties? Remember Monica's blue dress? This was priced at $49.95.

I'm not sure which, if any, information you gathered would be admissible in court or even legal to obtain in your state! You might be able to find out online under a search for divorce laws in your state. If you couldn't find out that way, you should ask an attorney. If you can afford to, hire a private investigator to do the work for you. They should know the laws and procure the proof you need through legal means.

You're probably thinking that by writing about ways you can catch a cheating partner, I'm also alerting the cheater to those ways, too. That's true, but if the cheater is concerned, he could find this information elsewhere.

So, my broken-hearted friends, BEFORE you begin your quest for the truth, check the laws in your state! And BEFORE you confront him, get the evidence!

Should I Trust Him?

We all know that in order to have a good relationship, we must have trust, right? But how much trust? If we trust 100%, are we naïve? And if we are distrustful of someone we love, does that mean we are jealous, or does it mean we are mindful of clues that are telling us something isn't right?

Call me 'jaded' if you like, but it's my opinion that having complete trust is naïve. After everything I've been through and seen, I'd be stupid if I trusted anyone. Humans are, by nature, going to let us down. People lie. I heard somewhere that men lie on average seven or eight times a day, and women lie approximately half as many times. Of course, no one knows for sure. Some may not lie at all, and some may lie practically from the time they wake, until they go to sleep. I've known a few of the latter. You know the type... if his lips are moving, he's lying.

I had a therapist tell me once that everyone lies. I have to agree, because even though I make a point of not ever lying, I'm not going to tell my mom that I don't like her chili, or tell my co-worker that her new jeans make her look like the broad side of a barn. I also won't go on about how good something looks if I don't like it. I usually don't mention it, but if I'm pressed, I try to be as vague as possible, avoiding an outright lie. But any deception is still a lie.

I'm not a fan of 'brutal truth.' I mean, it's not okay to say something cruel or hurtful to someone just because it's true. The fact that it's true doesn't warrant being mean. But that's not what I'm talking about here. What I'm talking about is relationship issues.

Unless you're 12 years old, and you're entering your first 'relationship,' there are going to be things you've experienced in the past with other people. It's not necessary, nor is it wise, to share with your current partner every intimate detail of what you experienced with someone else. Some things are private and are better kept that way. But other issues from the past are relevant to your current relationship.

For instance, if either of you have been married before, lived with someone before, had a lot of partners, have a history of being unfaithful, have or have had STDs.... I believe your current partner has the right to know those kinds of things. Also, if you have children from a previous relationship, your current partner not only has the right to know about the children, but also about the type of relationship you had and still have with the children's other parent.

The way to decide what should be disclosed is to decide whether or not the information would be needed or desired by someone you're with, in order to determine whether or not to develop or continue a relationship with you. If you would like to have that information from him, there's a good chance your partner would like to have it from you. If this information is asked of you, it's crucial that you be HONEST and that you share any other issues that could impact your relationship. Dishonesty could doom it right from the beginning.

Remember that once you lie, your partner probably won't ever completely trust you again. From the moment he realizes you've lied, everything you do or say will be suspect. You've proven that you're not trustworthy, and it's not the fault of the person you lied to that you aren't trusted. It's your own fault for not being honest.

So if there have been lies or some form of deception in your relationship, can trust be reestablished? That depends upon the person to whom you lied, what you lied about, and how many times you lied. It also depends upon the lengths to which you are willing to go to regain that person's trust. We all feel the need for privacy, but if you're not doing something that would hurt your partner, why would you care if he reads your email or texts? Why would you mind if he opens your mail? If he's the one who lied or cheated, and he's trying to make it right with you, why would he mind if you read his texts, mail, or email?

Some people feel justified in their lies, because they say the person to whom they are lying "can't handle the truth." But *why* can't this person handle the truth? Usually, people lie to hide things they are doing that they know will hurt the person they supposedly care for (or to keep from getting into trouble). So instead of modifying their behavior to avoid hurting someone they love, they do whatever they want to do, and then they lie about it and excuse the lies when they get caught by saying they didn't want to argue or to hurt you. "You were going to be livid about it, so I figured I'd avoid the fight until you found out and deal with it then." The truth is that they're hoping and praying you don't ever find out.

Okay, saying you think your neighbor is "average-looking" when you think he's really cute is one thing. It's a lie, and it's wrong. But if a guy says he's on a business trip when he's actually holed up with his lover, that's something else. A lie is a lie, but when you've been unfaithful, you've taken deception to a whole new level. Infidelity is a betrayal that takes much more work to get past than any other kind of deception. It takes counseling, forgiveness, God, and a huge effort on the part of the deceiver to be completely transparent.

If you're trying to regain a person's trust, you must be an open book. And if you need to talk to him 20 times a day, so you feel that he's where he's supposed to be and that he's being honest and open with you, then he should go along with that. After a while, it'll get old, but also, a bit of trust will reappear. However, if it takes a long time, he should remind himself that you're checking up on him because of his own deception and betrayal. If he tries to punish you for not trusting him after he's lied to and cheated on you, he's being unfair. Distrust is the price he has to pay for hurting you that way if he wants to hold onto the relationship.

But I must **warn** you here. If you've decided to stay with someone who has been unfaithful, don't be naïve! Don't think the affair or fling is over just because he promises or swears it is. Don't think you can trust him again, because he's sending you flowers or bringing you gifts. I know that you want to believe him, but keep your guard up and your eyes open. Check up on him. Make sure he's where he says he is. If he has nothing to hide, and he wants to save your relationship, he shouldn't have a problem with your making sure he's being honest.

Now, don't shoot the messenger. I hate to be the Grinch, but I have to tell it like it is. I'm not saying that relationships can't work after affairs. Some do. I'm just saying that it's hard to make them work even *before* an affair, and it's always infinitely more difficult afterward. Most people don't want to put in the effort it takes to make a relationship work. Especially when there are blended families, the stress and complications can really take a toll. But regardless of your situation, deception of any kind is like a disease. It grows, and it destroys the union, and if it isn't treated, the love won't survive.

If deception is or has been an issue between you and your partner, take it to a therapist. And remember that relationships suffering from deception have a much higher survival rate if caught and treated early. Don't wait. Get help now.

Chapter 3

The Cheater

The word *cheater* alone causes a visceral response in those of us who have been betrayed by one, and we all know the reason for this. It's because the act of cheating, being unfaithful in a supposedly monogamous relationship, causes a great deal of pain to everyone involved.

We think we know the cheater, but we actually know the stereotype (that is, unless you are a cheater). Most of us think of him as a mindless, heartless sex machine with no emotions, morals, or concern for anyone else. A walking, talking bag of testosterone—the sex drive hormone, also in females—in search of a hook-up. There are some people who might almost fit that description... or so it seems. But really, that's sort of a caricature.

When God created man, He told him to "be fruitful and multiply." In the Old Testament days, men had hundreds of wives, then they had their concubines, and they also had sex with prostitutes! The Bible says it's better for a man to put 'his seed' into a prostitute than to spill it onto the ground. My point is that in the beginning, God *wanted* them to be with different women to populate the Earth.

Obviously, underpopulation is no longer an issue, but that doesn't change what I believe God put into man's DNA. When the laws were changed, and man was supposed to go from having hundreds of women all the time, to having only one woman for the rest of his life, can you imagine the reaction? It was great for the one woman, but I'm sure the men were like, "Dude! You can't be serious!" I can see the shock on their faces now. Makes me laugh!

Please don't misunderstand what I'm saying. I'm NOT suggesting that makes cheating all right. In fact, adultery is the only acceptable reason given in the Bible for divorce, so that tells you how serious it is. What I am saying is that being faithful to one person is something that men have to really work on. It doesn't come naturally to us. It's much easier to sin than to not, but additionally, men (and women, to some degree) seem to be programmed to cheat. Even so, no one should have to deal with a man who doesn't respect her and love her enough to control his carnal appetite for other women.

There are many reasons why people are unfaithful. Below, you'll find descriptions of some of the types of cheaters I've encountered. I've given them labels that fit their particular sets of circumstances.

The Serial Cheater

The *serial cheater* sometimes doesn't even pretend to be in a monogamous relationship. He's commitment-phobic and immature. Most have been 'stuck' in unhappy relationships or been hurt in them. Sometimes it's instilled in him as a child, seeing adults in his life go through spouse after spouse, cheating, leaving, starting over, and cheating again. He is taught to cheat, and he sees it as the norm. He knows it's not right, but it still seems okay to him.

The Entitled Cheater

The *entitled cheater* loves his partner. He might be happy in his relationship. Or he might be bored, but still fairly content. He doesn't want out, but he feels entitled to have something exciting on the side. He needs to think about the consequences of his desire for fun and stop thinking that he's too smart to get caught. He almost always does get caught, and then he whines and begs to hold onto his partner, crying, "It didn't mean anything, I swear! It was just sex!" Hello! It was sex with someone other than your partner! How did you think she would feel? Right… she wasn't supposed to know. Well, you can't depend on that, so avoid the temptation!

The Accidental Cheater

And then there's the *accidental cheater*. He's usually a decent guy, with good morals, who would never have imagined he would cheat on a girlfriend, much less commit adultery. The accidental cheater has every intention of avoiding temptation, but somehow it sneaks up on him. He tries to resist, and he might succeed for a while, but then the circumstances are such that the temptation is overwhelming. He seems to think there is no way out (but there *always* is), so he gives in.

I'm NOT implying that he is somehow forced or coerced into the act. I mean that he succumbs to an all-consuming desire of his own volition.

Immediately, he is racked with guilt and feels horrible about himself and about what he did. These people usually only have one-nighters, but they can also fall into the trap of having an affair. If so, they're miserable, because they know the damage that what they are doing can cause.

The Whiny Cheater

Let's not forget the *whiny cheater*. He's in a relationship in which his partner has changed so much (according to him) that he feels he's justified in his cheating. He says, "She's not the woman I married. She got fat, and she wears ugly clothes." Yeah, it's lame, but you have to admit that there is some validity there. I mean, we all change as we age. We gain weight, we lose hair, some gain hair…. We aren't the same that we were in the beginning of the relationship, which is why it's important that we try to hold onto the love we once had by reconnecting and rekindling it if it's waned. Though there might be some valid points as to the change in a partner, that is NOT a license to cheat. If you can't be faithful to your partner because she isn't exactly like she was when you met her, do her a favor, and let her go.

The Good Guy Cheater

The *good guy cheater* is the one who has been in a crippled or dying marriage or relationship for a long time, maybe many years, and is still trying to accept it, rather than to leave. There is no real connection, because there is no intimacy. No caring, no affection, and no sex.

Well, there might be some sex, but it's cold and mechanical and completely unfulfilling—even disappointing. The dysfunction and the rejection by his partner have damaged his self-esteem so that he feels like he doesn't deserve anything better. He tells himself that he's staying for the benefit of their children, but instead of seeing a loving, healthy marriage, they see bitterness and arguments, without affection. He's teaching his children that's what a marriage looks like. He's on the floor emotionally. He's vulnerable, and he's looking. Then he meets someone. She's interested in him. She wants him. He can't resist. He agonizes over his decision, but then he leaves. Granted, he should've left before he entered into a relationship with another woman, but he never intended to leave.

The Revenge Cheater

It's not hard to figure out what the *revenge cheater* is all about. He wants to get back at his partner either for cheating or some other wrong, whether real or perceived. He feels hurt and angry, and he wants to hurt his partner to even the score. He's lashing out. His heart is probably not involved with the other woman at all, but if he isn't careful, that could change. He's vulnerable, and his need for revenge could be the downfall of his relationship with his partner.

In addition to those types of cheaters and situations, there are another couple of things that could cause a person to cheat. One is sex addiction. Another is bipolar disorder. Sometimes, during the manic phase of the illness, bipolar patients make poor choices, one of which is having multiple sexual partners. Both of these conditions should be monitored by a psychiatrist and a therapist and may require medication.

Like any group of people, cheaters are not all the same, and I can't list every type of cheater. There are many combinations of reasons and personalities. We might picture them all as monsters if we've been hurt by them, but they're people, too, even if we don't think of them that way. Most cheaters are not the mindless, heartless people we imagine them to be. Most of them do care about the pain they create, and they hate that their actions have caused others to suffer. But they're usually people who tend to focus mainly on themselves, so thoughts of the effects on others get pushed to the backs of their minds.

If your man is a cheater, and you've decided to stay with him, it's a good idea to take a look at the cheater and the relationship. (Refer back to **Why Did He Cheat?** and **Can I Prevent His Cheating?** in Chapter 1.)

No one deserves to be hurt, and that includes you.

Cheater Confessions

I'm including this section, because I think it's good to have the story from the horse's mouth, so to speak. It gives you some insight into the way cheaters think. So here are a few words from some of the 'horses' I'm familiar with.

First, I'd like to reiterate that obviously, cheating is wrong, no matter what the reasons. With that being said, for the hundredth time, there are certain circumstances that kinda, sorta, *almost* justify cheating, though not quite. As you might imagine, I was in one of those circumstances.

As I told you, I was in an abusive relationship for seven years with a cheating man who was a drug addict and alcoholic. Yeah, I could pick 'em, right? I tried for a long time to get away from him, but he wouldn't let me go. He kept tricking me into thinking things would be different, and especially since I was young, I really wanted to believe what he said. I wasn't cynical enough at the time to know better.

I was afraid, and I didn't have the courage to go out on my own, so my cheating was an attempt to find a way out of the misery of life with that man. I didn't intend to stay with him. Even so, I was consumed with guilt, and I was terrified that he would find out. Though he tormented me physically, emotionally, and in every other way conceivable, I still didn't want to hurt him. That's amazing, when you consider the fact that he cheated on me throughout our entire relationship.

It was exciting to be with someone else, but not because I was cheating. I didn't like that part. It was because it's always thrilling to find someone new whom you really like and with whom you have a strong chemistry. The cheating made me feel sick, nervous, and dirty.

I was miserable in that situation. I had no self-esteem, and I was hoping for a way out, so I could find a better life.

Finally, I was able to do that, and I'll admit that the encouragement and support of another man did help me gain the strength I needed to leave that nightmare. I know it was wrong, and I do wish I could've handled things differently, but I did what I had to do at the time.

Okay, now for the guys. Some of them were strictly friends, and others, I knew more intimately. The following is a compilation of remarks and points of view that I've heard from different men regarding their cheating:

* "I love my wife, and I'll never leave her, but I just want some fun on the side."

* "I don't love my wife, but I love my kids, and I can't leave them. I just need some female attention."
That one left his wife.

* "Getting some *strange* is such a rush."

* "You start feeling like you're not a man. Like what makes you attractive is gone, and then a good-looking woman gives you some attention, and you just can't resist it."

* "I never meant to get involved with anyone else, but we met and became friends, and it just snow-balled from there. I fell for her, and I didn't allow myself to think about what was best for anyone else."

* "I'm trying to get my finances in order, so I can get out and start a new life. I've never really loved a woman. I want to fall in love."
About a month later, that guy was driving a new red sports car. He was seeing several different women at the time. He eventually divorced and married his children's nanny.

* "We got married so young, I never really got a chance to sew my wild oats."
Also quoted from the sports-car-driving nanny lover.

* "She cheated on me and broke my heart before we got married, so I figure it's my turn now."
He left his wife, remarried, left that wife for another woman, and is still living with that one.

* "She won't give me what I want and need at home, so why shouldn't I get it somewhere else?"

* "I'm not a bad guy. I'm not looking for a way out of my marriage. I'm just really bored and horny."

* "My wife is not into sex as much as I am. Her drive is really low, and I need it way more than she does."

* "My wife doesn't like to do the kinds of things I like. She's very reserved."

* "I've offered my wife everything from cruises to mink coats if she'll go down and swallow, but she won't do it."
This one finally got caught in a relationship with one of his other women, but his wife stayed with him.

* "My wife would never understand my fantasies. I'm too ashamed to share them with her, so that's why I cheat. I'm not so inhibited with anyone else."

There was one guy I knew years ago who said that when he cheated, the fear of getting caught was part of the excitement for him. He said the rush was like right before an addict (which he was) is about to take a hard drug—it's overwhelming. I asked him if it were like actually *doing* the drug, and he said, "Not like smoking pot. But definitely like shooting up—like slamming coke."

Drug and alcohol addicts are sometimes also sex addicts, or at least, serial cheaters. That kind of personality is easily addicted to the rush of endorphins we receive when we begin a romantic and/or sexual relationship with someone new. When the novelty begins to wear off, they have to move on to someone else who can give them their fix. So in many cases, it's not necessarily the sex per se that the person is addicted to—it's the endorphin rush they get from the interaction and the prospect of having sex.

Another aspect of that type of relationship that is important to ponder is, like I said, sometimes it's the *prospect* of having sex with someone new that the guy gets so excited about. Once he's conquered her, much of the thrill is gone, unless she makes it difficult for him to be with her again.

So much with regard to sex is like a game for men. It's the challenge that they love. If it comes too easily for them, they don't appreciate it. They need to have to work for it. I've even heard men say that.

The only thing I can imagine that *might* keep a man like that interested is having some serious spice going on at home. However, even with that, I don't think a serial cheater will ever be able to resist temptation. It's an addiction that they don't want to recover from. They enjoy it way too much. They're like meth addicts, only worse!

Married Men & Female Friends

You see your man talking to a gorgeous woman, and they seem to be enjoying the conversation, not to mention each other. When you get the chance to ask him about her, he says, "We're just friends!"

Remember in *When Harry Met Sally*, Harry explained that men and women couldn't really be friends? He said something to the effect that men always wanted to have sex with attractive women, so the friendship always fails.

Harry's explanation might be slightly exaggerated, but I think it's pretty much on the mark. And it goes both ways. There are also plenty of women who have male 'friends' whom they would like nothing more than to have as lovers. The difference is that the women could probably get the guys into bed, but then they would lose them as friends, because the weirdness would creep in.

There's no way to get accurate statistics about such things as infidelity, but I will tell you that many affairs begin as friendships. Okay, notice that I *didn't* say 'one-nighters' or 'flings.' I said 'affairs.' The reason I am differentiating between affairs and casual sex is that people who genuinely care for each other, as real friends do, don't normally use each other strictly for sex, though I'm sure it does work for some. Real friends develop deep concern for each other, which can easily go from being an innocent friendship, to infatuation, to a full-blown love affair in a fairly short period of time.

So you think your partner has a platonic friendship with a woman? Don't let the fact that she's not Angelina Jolie give you a false sense of security. When people connect on other levels, the looks are not quite as important. For example, I had a family member who had an affair with a woman who was less attractive, not nearly as intelligent, and much less successful than his wife. For whatever reason, the other woman made him feel good about himself. Men (and women) with low self-esteem are particularly vulnerable and are easily attracted to people who are less physically appealing, which makes them feel better about themselves.

You have even more reason to be suspicious if your man has been intimately involved with his female friend before. There's that 'knowing.' I think you know what I mean—the memories. He'll probably never admit it, but if they are still close enough to be 'friends,' he still thinks of her sexually. When he looks at her, he remembers things they did together in bed. Don't bother asking him, though. He'll deny it and tell you that you're crazy.

I know a guy who used to have his former girlfriend and her husband over to his house to cook out and play cards with his wife. And he and his ex were still sexually involved! And his wife *knew* they had lived together before! He said that he got a big thrill out of knowing his wife and the other woman's husband were right there, and he and Blondie were getting away with their fling right under the noses of their spouses. I would have to guess that his wife felt as if she were strong and open minded, allowing their 'friendship.' If she had known the things they were doing behind her back, she wouldn't have been so accepting of little Miss Blondie.

A woman I know did the same thing, only it wasn't with an ex. She was having an affair with a guy, and she would have him and his wife over for dinner with her and her husband. I asked her how that didn't freak her out—how she could do it. She said it didn't bother her at all. They were all friends, and they had fun together.

I can't imagine having the nerve to do something like that. I cringe at the thought that my husband might *accidentally* meet guys I dated years before he and I got together, whom I'm NOT involved with now! It's uncomfortable for me—not exciting. It's scary. It makes me nervous to even think about it.

I believe the most dangerous place for a committed relationship or marriage is probably the workplace. When two people who have a sexual attraction for each other work together, it's extremely difficult to control because of the repeated contact they have. If they work closely together, it's a recipe for disaster. It's almost impossible to control.

If you think I'm trying to scare you, you're right. I don't want you to condone a so-called friendship that might start out as a "harmless flirtation" or business contact, but end up as something that will damage, or even destroy, your relationship.

When your partner tells you, "I'm not attracted to her! There's nothing going on," don't trust it. I used to think physical attraction was something that was either there or it wasn't. I thought it couldn't be cultivated. I learned that I was wrong about that.

Years ago, I met a guy through a mutual friend. He was nice, and he made me laugh, but I wasn't attracted to him physically at all. The only attraction I felt for him was as a friend. However, over a period of months, we went from small talk, to brief conversations. From there, we developed trust and friendship.

After a few more months, things took a turn. He said he wanted to *show* me how much he loved me. Looking back, I know that I should've seen it coming, but I didn't. I was really shocked. But he was good to me in many ways and made me feel better about myself, so I got involved with him. Eventually, I fell in love with him.

Okay, I said all that to make this point: I started out with absolutely no attraction to that guy, to being completely drawn to him. So even if your man doesn't find his friend sexually appealing now, that doesn't mean he won't sometime in the near future. After he gets to know her better, that interest might develop. Or the relationship might be platonic now, because she isn't drawn to him sexually. But if she were to become vulnerable, she might develop an attraction to him. And naturally, the same could be said about your own feelings for an opposite-sex friend.

I'm not going to say that it's impossible to have a platonic male-female relationship, or that if your man has a female friend, he's definitely sleeping with her. But I will say that if your guy has a female friend, and especially if she's pretty, you'd better not turn a blind eye to it. Even if she's also your friend, if your man talks to her or sees her without your being there, you have good reason to be suspicious. I've seen it too many times. Don't trust it!

Influenced to Cheat

Have you ever been influenced to cheat? I've seen that happen with men, and I'm sure it also occurs with some women. It's like dog pack behavior. A guy who might be able to resist temptation if he were alone is not so likely to be a good boy when surrounded by his cheating friends.

If you're married or in a committed relationship, you should think about the people with whom you spend time. Not only are you (sometimes unfairly) judged by the company you keep, but you're probably at least somewhat also influenced by them.

If you're concerned about your relationship, you might want to rethink whom you are associating with if they are the type of people who are unfaithful to their partners. It's not that you are *unable* to stick to your morals when you're with them. It's just that when surrounded by people who are participating in that type of behavior, it doesn't seem as wrong as it would if you were alone or with other friends. It begins to seem normal, and therefore, not something you would feel as bad about doing.

That's why it's not a good idea for married people to go out, without their partners, with friends who are single. The single people are trying to hook up, and the married people are tempted, and maybe even encouraged, to do it. It takes a very strong person to be in a club or bar atmosphere, where lots of testosterone is flowing, and not do things that his partner would consider cheating. It's like playing Russian Roulette. If you play it long enough, you're bound to lose. Why subject yourself to that kind of temptation when you know the possible consequences?

And don't think I'm giving those people a pass on their infidelity. Just because you've made bad choices regarding the people you spend time with doesn't mean you aren't responsible for your own actions. That choice to be with them is also your responsibility. You knew what you were doing and what could happen. It's not your friends' fault if you cheat. It's your own fault, so don't try to blame them.

I know you'd miss hanging with your friends, but rather than going to a club, meet them for lunch or maybe a game of golf. You don't golf? Well, be creative. There are things you can do that don't involve cheating. Have some friends over to watch a football or basketball game. Meet at a friend's house to have a beer and play some pool. Shoot some hoops.

Ladies, we're good at all the other stuff—shopping, going to the salon, just hanging out at home and talking…. If you want to avoid infidelity, you have to be smart about the places you go, the people with whom you surround yourself, and the things you do when you're away from your partner.

It's not an accident that some people are faithful. It's a choice they've made. They chose to put their partners first, rather than their friends. Friends are important, but when they are more important than your partner, you're asking for trouble.

If you're in a relationship that's important to you, think about the influence your friends, acquaintances, and coworkers have on you and the way you behave when you're with them. If you're more disposed to be unfaithful when you're with them, maybe you should be looking for some new friends.

Taking Responsibility

Passing the buck seems to be the way people handle every situation in which they find themselves in trouble. No one wants to take responsibility for his own actions. It's always someone else's fault, or he wouldn't have cheated if someone else hadn't done something to tempt him, or some such garbage. Give me a break!

It's difficult to claim responsibility for things we do that make us feel ashamed and embarrassed. It's much easier to blame someone else or make excuses for our actions. I understand that. But I also understand that if you're capable of having sex outside your relationship, you should be big enough to take responsibility for it.

Men, if you love your partners, and you want to stay with them, do not get involved with other women! Just don't! But if you do, don't blame the women with whom you cheat! Be strong and mature enough to admit that you made a mistake and that no one else is to blame. I mean, if you aren't honest enough to say, "Okay, I screwed up. I'm sorry. Please forgive me, and I'll do my best to make it up to you from now on," why should your partner give you another chance?

Sometimes it isn't only the guilty party who makes the excuses. When it comes to infidelity, the partner of the cheating man almost always buys into the idea that the other woman is responsible for her man's infidelity. She takes that ball and runs with it! She tells everyone she knows about how that woman relentlessly threw herself at him until he just couldn't resist her anymore. Nonsense!

Do you think your man would be so quick to let you off the hook if you cheated on him? Obviously, he'd want to beat the other man senseless, but that's a matter of pride. Do you think he would pin the whole thing on your lover, rather than holding you accountable for what you chose to do? There might be a handful of guys like that, but not many.

Girls, think about this. What do you really think of a man who blames someone else for his own bad decisions? How would you feel about him if he were blaming you for something he did wrong, which he might do? Do you respect weakness and immaturity? What about respect for yourself? Do you think you deserve to be with a man who is unfaithful to you and doesn't even have the decency to admit he made a mistake? What kind of man can't take responsibility for his own actions and blames a person that HE brought into the situation?

How can you defend a man like that? If you're blaming the one he cheated *with*, that's what you're doing—defending him. How can you believe anything he says? How can you trust him? Why would you *want* to trust him?

He put his own sexual pleasure above your wellbeing. He decided that getting off with someone else was more important than protecting you from being hurt. By shielding him from taking responsibility for what he did to you, you're taking his side! You might as well tell him that what he did was okay. Why would you do that?

49

First of all, you don't have to be a genius to know that no woman can force a man to have sex with her. If a man has sex, he does it because he wants to, regardless of what he might tell you. That's what most people call 'common sense.' I don't call it that, because it's actually logic, and thinking that way is not so common. Logic tells us that men aren't jumping into bed with women against their own will. They are acting of their own volition. They enjoy it, so they do it. So how is anyone other than the cheater responsible for his conscious choice to be unfaithful to you?

This is a subject about which people feel strongly. I understand what it feels like to have a man be unfaithful to you. It hurts like crazy. And I understand that you love him, and you're looking for a way to avoid blaming him. That's the only way you can justify staying with someone who chose being with someone else over preserving his relationship with you. But should you do that?

Look at it this way: Say you have two little boys. The older one does something wrong, and the younger one goes along with it. You give the older boy a hug and tell him to sit down and eat. You send the younger boy to bed without dinner, because he took part in the older boy's misbehavior. Does that seem fair? Does it even make any sense? NO! It's ridiculous!

But blaming the woman with whom your husband cheated, while holding onto him and holding him blameless, is basically the same thing. She went along with his sin (IF she even knew he was married), but *he* is the one who broke his vows. *He* is responsible for his actions, but you aren't holding him accountable. Instead, you're blaming her for something *he* did.

When we feel ashamed about something we do, we sometimes try to defend or minimize it. But strong, mature, responsible people stand up and claim the blame for their own actions. They don't pass the buck on to someone else.

If I didn't love my husband, and I refused to meet his needs, and he found another woman who did meet his needs, I would feel *a bit* of responsibility for his infidelity. But ultimately, it would be his choice, and his actions would be his own.

My first husband cheated on me regularly, and he abused me physically, emotionally, and sexually. Even so, when I cheated on him, I was wrong. When I was involved with a man who was separated or married, regardless of what he told me, or didn't tell me, or why he was cheating, I was wrong in being with him. I take responsibility for my own actions. **BUT I WILL NOT TAKE RESPONSIBILITY FOR HIS ACTIONS**, just as I wouldn't have blamed the guys with whom I cheated in my first marriage. It wasn't their fault that I chose to cheat, because I was too weak and afraid to leave my abuser. They weren't responsible for my actions, and I'm not responsible for anyone else's actions.

Most people quickly jump to accept praise for their accomplishments, and that's fine. However, when it comes to taking the blame for their own mistakes, they aren't so willing to step up. I think that's usually due to fear. They don't want to face the consequences of their actions. But we all make mistakes. None of us is perfect. I'm not suggesting that any of us throw stones! We need to try to be understanding and forgiving, which is the whole purpose of this book. But remember that being understanding and forgiving doesn't mean that you have to stay with the person who hurts you. That's a choice you have to make.

Those who claim responsibility for their mistakes are much more likely to be respected than those who try to throw someone else under the bus. If you did it, own it, and try to make amends. That's the only way you'll ever be able to reestablish any trust. There's no guarantee, but it's worth a try.

The Cheater & Domestic Violence

Domestic violence and infidelity are not always linked, but it's pretty common. This is probably because cheating and domestic violence both involve a lack of respect for women and an inability or unwillingness to control one's own actions. The types of personalities that behave this way are similar, if not the same.

Lack of self-control is a key component in domestic violence. While some men feel entitled to treat women any way they choose, including battering them, most men know that their behavior is unacceptable, to say the least. They deny allegations of abuse, and they try to hide their behavior from friends and family.

The same is usually true about cheaters. Some men might feel as if there is nothing wrong with cheating, but most know better and even feel bad about the effects of their infidelity on their partners and children—yet they still do it.

Men who perpetrate domestic violence are more than just disrespectful of women, however. They are usually misogynists, men who hate women. They despise their own need to have the love and companionship of a woman, and one of the ways they try to cope with those feelings is that they have different lovers in order to keep from getting too close to one woman. It helps them to keep a sense of distance between themselves and their partners.

Domestic violence not only manifests itself physically. Emotional and sexual abuse can also be violent and sometimes more painful than being battered. Cheating is one of the ways a man can hurt a woman and degrade her, making her feel less important to him than she really is. His thinking is that in allowing her to know he is desired by other women, it will make her hold onto him. It sounds crazy, because it is, but amazingly enough, many times, it works. That was one of my ex's favorite tools.

Abusers, as well as cheaters, have a tendency to blame their victims. After breaking a woman's nose, her husband might say, "Look what you did! Why do you make me do this to you?" Cheaters defend their actions in their own minds, too. It's not uncommon for a cheater to say something like, "You don't give me what I want, so it's your fault that I had to get it somewhere else." One of my abusers used to say to me, "I would treat you like a queen if you would just let me!" In other words, "It's your fault that I just knocked you across the room."

There's no way to tip-toe around the fact that this is a terribly dysfunctional type of relationship. Whether you're being battered or not, if your partner doesn't care enough about you to treat you with respect, you need to get help. If you can't afford a psychiatrist, call your local Mental Health Center. If you can't afford treatment, and you qualify, they will treat you on a sliding scale. And I'm not suggesting that you need to be medicated—to the contrary. I'm just saying that if you are in an abusive or otherwise dysfunctional relationship, there are reasons. It's not an accident, and you need to find out what's going on with you that caused you to become involved with the kind of person who would treat you this way.

If nothing else, your self-esteem is very low. Speaking with a therapist can be extremely helpful in getting you to realize your own potential and the fact that you do not deserve to be battered or abused in any way. You also do not deserve to have someone cheat on you. No matter what your flaws, mistakes, or other excuses he might dream up, you deserve better. Getting some therapy can help you to respect yourself enough to do whatever is necessary to make life better for yourself and your children.

Life is too short. Don't allow yourself to be beaten down either physically, emotionally, or otherwise by someone you think loves you. We all want to be loved, but regardless of what he says, any man who would abuse you or cheat on you doesn't truly love you. The way I see it is, "If that's love, I don't want any part of it!"

I know how you feel. I've been slapped. I've been punched. I've been strangled. I've been kicked. I've had thick bunches of my hair pulled out. I've been shaken so hard that it felt like my head would explode. I've been thrown to the floor. I've been raped. I've been mocked. I've been called stupid, fat, and every kind of bitch and slut (among other things) you can imagine. And I've been cheated on. It all hurts equally. And it takes a lot of strength to get away, but with help, you can do it. I might not have ever had the strength to get away from the men who abused me if it weren't for my getting therapy. And I'm sure I would be dead if I had stayed with them.

The men who abuse you and cheat on you will try to make you think you deserve the way they treat you. They'll tell you that no one else would ever treat you any better, because you're a bitch, a slut, a sorry lay, etc. Don't believe their lies!

I stayed with one guy, because I thought that if I left him, I'd find another guy like him, and it wasn't worth the hassle. But that was many years ago. Now, I'm married to a man who loves me and says he wouldn't ever hit me. We've been together for seven years, and so far, he hasn't. It's not perfect, but it's pretty good overall.

That can happen for you, too, but not if you stay with your abuser. Do whatever it takes to get away from him. Tell your family and friends. Call the Mental Health Center. Find a support group. You can do it. And you will do it, because you're awesome! You just don't realize it yet.

Advice for the Cheater

As I stated before, there are many reasons why people are unfaithful to their partners. I have a few words to address specific issues, but in general, I have to say this: Use condoms! And take a minute to stop and look at what you're doing!

If you're a *serial cheater*, ask yourself why. I've heard guys call themselves 'players' and say things like, "I can't be tied down, because I love women. Gotta spread the love."

That's not love. It's sex. I'm sure you know there's a difference. There is no love involved when you treat women as your playthings, lying to them, making them think you care, while you're doing the same with other women. What's a game to you is actually someone else's life. Do you think it's fair to play with women's hearts and cause turmoil and pain in their lives?

Would it be fair for a woman to treat you, your brother, or your son that way? That would make her a 'slut' or a 'ho,' right? What does it make you when you do it to them? A man whore! You might think that's cool, but the only people who would agree with you are others like you. To everyone else, it's disgusting.

You might see yourself as a gift to the women of the world, but in reality, you are much more their nightmare than their dream. You get annoyed by women who try to establish a relationship when they develop feelings for you, because they cramp your style. Well, if you're too immature to have an adult relationship, don't pretend to care, and don't see the same woman more than once. Be straightforward about the fact that you are not mature enough to commit to anyone and that you don't want a relationship.

As crazy as it sounds, you will still get laid. There are women who will take that as a challenge, or feel sorry for you, and they will have sex

54

with you. But at least, they'll have some idea of what they're getting into. My best advice to you is to grow up and get some therapy.

To the *entitled cheater*, I have to ask you these questions: What makes you think you're entitled to have more than one woman? Why do you think that's okay for you? And do you really think that having meaningless sex with another woman is something your partner should get over and forget about?

Put yourself in your partner's place. How would you feel if the woman you "love" had a history of cheating on you? She does it because she can—because you let it slide. You allow it, because she says it doesn't mean anything, so you're okay with it. Ridiculous, right? Insane? Not in a million years, you say? I hear ya. It wouldn't be okay for her to do what you're doing, so why is it okay for you? It's not. Think about her feelings. Think about how you would feel if she were doing what you're doing. She's not entitled to be with others. Neither are you.

Mr. *Accidental Cheater*, you know what you need to do. You never intended to get into this mess. You know what's right, so just do it. I know you feel bad about what you're doing, so I suggest that you talk to a therapist. Maybe talk with your pastor or a church counselor before making a decision about whether or not to tell your partner. I think most women would want to know you cheated, but there are some who don't, especially if it were only a one-time thing. That's a choice *you* have to make.

Regardless of whether you tell her or not, the fling or affair has to end. Do what you have to do. And when faced with temptation again, do whatever it takes to avoid it. If she can't be avoided, because she's someone you work with, maybe you should look into a transfer or a new job. What good is a job if you lose the woman you love because of a sexual attraction to someone else?

If you're the *whiny cheater*, you know who you are. You have a hundred excuses for why you're cheating. She's fat, she cut her hair, she doesn't wear makeup anymore, she doesn't want sex anymore.... Shut up and look at yourself. Are you perfect? Do you look the same as you did when you got together? You might think you do, but maybe you don't.

One night, my husband and I were watching *The Sopranos*. Tony was walking around his kitchen in only a towel. I said, "How can he walk around on camera with that huge gut hanging out?" Kelley said, "He doesn't know it's there." I laughed so hard! He said, "I guarantee you, he has no idea his gut's that big." So maybe you're not as hot as you think, either.

So what if she gained weight? And maybe she doesn't want to make herself look good, or have sex with you, because of the way you treat her. Ever think of that? Maybe subconsciously, she's trying to make herself unattractive in a passive-aggressive way to punish you for cheating on her or hurting her in some other way.

This is the bottom line: If you don't want to be with her anymore, leave. But if you love her and want to have sex with her, or you want it to be better, you have the power to do that. You can be nice to her and make her feel good about herself. You can do things for her. You can try to make yourself more attractive for her. Take her out. Show her you love her. It'll make a huge difference in your relationship, and then in your sex life with her. If it doesn't, then talk with her about your concerns. If neither of you is willing to get therapy and try to make it work, maybe it's time to let it go. But don't continue the cheating. At least, have enough respect for yourself and your partner to wait to be with someone else until after you two are over.

As for the *good guy cheater*, it's simple. If your marriage or relationship is over, get out of it *before* you get involved with someone else. If you've already begun another relationship, don't continue to stay in the dead relationship, thinking it's the right thing to do. Cheating is never the right thing. If you can stay in the marriage or relationship and not be unfaithful, that's okay. It's up to you. But you aren't doing anyone any favors by staying and cheating. It's unfair to everyone involved, including your children. (See **The Children** in Chapter 7.)

Revenge cheater, do you feel better? Is hurting your partner really helping you? I know you feel justified, especially if she cheated first, but all you're doing is muddying the waters. If you love your partner, try to work it out. If you've cheated, consider the score settled. Forgive and ask to be forgiven.

If you get some couples counseling, maybe you can fix what's been broken. If not, please don't stay in the broken relationship, one-upping each other, wasting precious years of your lives. Let go and move on.

Now, to all cheaters, I want to say this: If you love the other woman so much that you can't let her go, you need to make a choice. It's not fair for you to hold onto both of them. It's selfish, and it's cruel. Man up and make a decision. Choose which one you want to be with, and cut the other loose. Allow her to grieve, get over you, and get on with her life. That's the best thing you could do for both of them. Provide for your ex, so your absence won't leave her unable to survive, but don't stay for the sake of security.

Guys, if you confess or get caught, be a man—not a sissy. Don't blame your other woman for your cheating. Deep down, you know she's not to blame, and it takes a coward to blame her for your decision to be unfaithful. How could any woman respect a man who doesn't have the balls (sorry) to stand up and admit that he made a mistake and wants to apologize and make amends for it? "I'm so sorry, baby, but she wouldn't leave me alone. She just kept on until I couldn't resist anymore." That's pathetic. Don't go there.

If you've cheated on a partner, please take a look at yourself and your actions. I say this not in judgment, but in love. I know that you have a heart and that you care about the feelings of those you love. If this is true, you want to stop this behavior, so you don't continue to hurt others, as well as yourself.

Please speak with a therapist. There are reasons why we do the things we do, and sometimes we're unaware of them. Speaking to a therapist can help you find a way to change your life for the better, not to mention the lives of those close to you. Take the step, and make that change. You'll be glad you did. And you won't have to worry about one of your women going all Lorena Bobbitt on you! If you don't know who Lorena Bobbitt is, I'd suggest you Google her.

Chapter 4

The Betrayed

Whether you saw it coming or you were blindsided, finding that your partner is cheating is absolutely gut wrenching. It's one of the most debilitatingly painful experiences anyone could ever have, always resulting in broken hearts—plural. I've often wished I had an 'off' button for my emotions. I bet you do, too.

Probably the first thing to cross your mind, after "I'm gonna kill him!" is "Why?" or "How could he do this to me?" You think of the time you've spent together, the children, the crises, the good times, the promises, the wedding vows....

Then you want to know who it is. If you find out (or even if you don't), your next thought is probably, "I'll kill her!" But wait a minute. Is that logical? I know, you don't care if it's logical. But do you really want to go to prison—or worse—for murder? And secondly, who was it that cheated on you? It wasn't her, was it? It was your partner. Don't lose focus on what has happened.

He cheated on you. *He* is the one who promised to love you, forsaking all others. *He* is the one who chose to get involved with someone else. *She* might not even know you exist!

I think that few of us are ever truly blindsided by infidelity. We have a feeling. We know it in our souls. Maybe it's women's intuition, but we just somehow know that something is not right. Your partner seems different. He seems distracted and uninterested in what's going on around him. He's watching a movie, and you ask him what it's about, but he doesn't seem to know. He's a million miles away... with her.

Women handle the infidelity of their men in different ways. Below, you'll see some of the different types of betrayed women that I've seen.

Butterfly

I had a friend who once told me that she didn't see anything she didn't want to see—anything that might bother her. She said, "I just live in my little Butterfly World, where everything is all happy and pretty." If a woman is ever really blindsided by infidelity, it seems that it would have to be a butterfly girl. I don't understand choosing to live in a fantasy world. My advice would be to wake the heck up and deal with reality.

Disinterested

Many betrayed partners know about the infidelity but choose not to acknowledge it. I call that *looking the other way*. She seems to be okay with the infidelity as long as he comes home at night, is a good father, and keeps the money coming in. She is usually one who has opted out of the relationship emotionally and is there is name only. She has other interests, possibly other relationships, and no longer wants a sexual or romantic relationship with her partner. She only expects him to be discreet in order to save face.

Denial

Other betrayed women are simply unable to accept the possibility that their partners could cheat. This type of woman sees the signs, but she is determined not to face them. She also looks the other way, but it's not because she doesn't care. It's because she is in denial. She refuses to believe what's going on right under her nose.

Terrified

Some betrayed partners care, and are not in denial, but keep quiet about the infidelity because they are afraid of losing their relationship with the cheater if they say or do anything about it. She silently agonizes over his cheating, hoping and praying that, like a monster in the dark, if she doesn't acknowledge it, it'll go away.

Crumbled

Still others are devastated and fall apart. This type is unable to function normally. She starts missing work and neglecting herself, the children, and the housework because of the intense pain and overwhelmingly deep depression. She tries desperately to hold onto her partner, because she has lost all self-esteem. Some even attempt suicide. Some succeed.

Postal

There are also those who 'go postal.' This woman turns her pain and sense of betrayal into rage. She vows to make him pay. She promises to get even. She immediately either leaves or forces the cheater to leave the home. She might become violent, attacking him physically or damaging his (or their) property. She might physically go after the other woman. She's through with him... but not really. Many times, this type of person carries that rage into the rest of her life, damaging or destroying all subsequent relationships.

These are only a few of the different types of behaviors of betrayed women. There are combinations of characteristics and personalities, as well as circumstances.

Blaming the Other Woman

Slut, whore, trash, homewrecker…. We've heard it all before, and some of us have even said things like that about the women our men have cheated with. But why is that? Have you ever thought about it? Why do so many people blame the other woman?

Don't flip out on me. I'm not saying that it's okay to be involved with another woman's man. *But why are we blaming the person the cheater cheated WITH, rather than blaming the cheater?*

Think about it. When you hear women talking about a man who cheated on his partner, what do they say? You might hear a bit of, "That sorry S.O.B," but then they immediately focus on the other woman. "She's nothing but trash." "She's a low-life slut." "I heard she's been with every guy in town that'll have her." "She needs her ass kicked." "You just wait till I get my hands on that little whore!"

How is it her fault that your man chose to cheat on you? Why is it her responsibility to see that your man is faithful to you? Why does she owe that to you? She doesn't!

The woman your man cheated with might not even know about you. As you probably all know well, cheaters don't tell the truth. They say whatever will get them through the moment with the least amount of resistance to what they want. If that means lying, they lie, especially when it comes to sex.

"Wife? Kids? Who, me? No, I'm single!" He's not wearing a ring, and he says he's not married, so are we supposed to know telepathically which men are married or in 'committed' relationships? That's asking a bit much, isn't it?

I've heard people say, "Well, you should Google anyone you're thinking of dating." Really? Okay, well, what if you do, and you don't see anything suspicious? Then what if he turns out to be married, with three children? Is that still your fault if you're dating him? Come on! He knows he's married, so *he's* the one who needs to stop it before it starts!

I've been thinking about this issue for a long time, because I'm amazed at the amount of hatred and rage that is directed toward the other woman. I've always heard it, but there was a moment one day, when I was watching a TV show, when it really dawned on me.

They had a woman on the show, and she was in tears. She had recently ended a long-term relationship with a married man. He had made all kinds of promises to her. You know, the standard, "I love you. I don't love her and haven't for a long time. There's no relationship there. We haven't slept together in years, and I don't want her. I want to be with you. I'm going to get a divorce and marry you…."

The poor woman was crying, obviously devastated by what that man had put her through. I felt so sorry for her. Then the audience was allowed to make comments or ask questions. Wow! I couldn't believe the way they all attacked her. It was crazy. And NO ONE said anything about the affair being the fault of the cheater! It was all her fault, even though *he* was the one who was cheating, lying, and breaking hearts!

One older woman in the audience stood up, and with rage written all over her face, she said, "If I could get a hold of you, I'd pull your hair and scratch your eyes out!" She didn't even know the woman on stage, but she wanted to physically attack her, because she had fallen for, and slept with, a married man.

The other audience members were saying things like, "Well, it's your own fault for being stupid enough to believe his lies," and "I don't care how much you cry! You got exactly what you deserved!" Again, she should've been psychic and known he was lying to her, right?

Women know what it's like to fall in love, and to love so deeply that you make yourself believe things you shouldn't. Haven't we all been there? It's second nature to us. You want to believe that the man you love is not a lying, cheating sack of…. Well, you get where I'm going with that. You want to believe it when he says he loves you and wants to marry you. We can imagine (if we haven't experienced) what it's like to be in a dead and loveless relationship and want something better for ourselves. So why should we judge them for being in that kind of situation, right? How are we supposed to know they're lying?

Maybe you're saying, "If you knew he was married, you should've never gotten involved! Or if you found out later, you should've ended it!" Hello! How about, ***HE SHOULDN'T HAVE STARTED IT***? *He's* the one who's married!

If only it were that simple. And you can say it's simple all you want, but that doesn't make it so. When dealing with matters of the heart, nothing is that simple. When you fall for a man, it's difficult, if not impossible, to be completely objective and make good decisions.

Again, you're trying to make decisions based upon what you think is true, when that information might be the farthest thing from the truth. You might decide to enter into (or continue) a relationship with a man you believe loves you and is in the middle of a divorce, when he's actually going home every night to his loving wife, trying to get her pregnant! How can you know that?

Everyone knows it would be wise to not enter into or continue a relationship with someone who is still legally married or is in a committed relationship, but when your heart gets involved, what's best begins to get lost in the fog of love and passion.

As I've said before, this is not to condone having a relationship with a married or otherwise committed person. That's NOT what I'm doing. And it's certainly not to upset or anger anyone. I'd never want to do that. The purpose of this book is to promote healing by understanding.

If you don't see the other woman as an all-powerful, cold-hearted monster who eats married men and their families for breakfast, you might be able to see that she is just a woman who's in a very painful, extremely bad situation. She made bad choices, many times based upon false information she believed to be true. She believed promises that we all want to believe—that someone loves her and wants to marry her.

Actually, there is a higher purpose for this section of the book, which is to make you understand that even though the woman who has been intimate with your partner might not ever be your friend, she's also not your enemy.

Remember, that woman didn't force your man to cheat on you. No one put a gun to his head. He is responsible for his own actions, including the ones that have caused you so much pain. I'm only asking that you put the blame where it should be—on the cheater. If your home is wrecked, it isn't that woman who wrecked it. The cheater is the homewrecker.

Ultimate Betrayal

Fortunately, in most cases of infidelity, the cheater gets involved with someone his partner doesn't know. In these cases, I'm always saying that the focus should be on the cheater, because he's the one who promised to be faithful, and yet he's the one who's hurting you. However, there are cases in which it makes sense to place equal blame upon the other woman. Those are the cases of ultimate betrayal.

I was watching Shania Twain talking on TV about her husband cheating on her. She was heartbroken, because her husband betrayed her, but the focus of her anger was on the other woman. Surprise! But in her case, it was fully warranted. Why? Because the other woman was her close friend—the woman in whom she was confiding about her problems with her husband.

In a case where the other woman is a friend or family member of the betrayed, not only is she betrayed by the cheater, but also by that woman who is supposed to care about her. In such an instance, both the cheater and the other woman are equally to blame, because they both have a relationship with the betrayed and should've both been concerned for her feelings enough to avoid getting into a situation where an intimate relationship could develop.

You can say that a total stranger should also take into account the feelings of the partner of the man she loves, or with whom she is sexually and/or romantically involved, and that's true. But how much more should she consider the feelings of a friend or family member?

In Shania's case, the husband of her friend told Shania about the affair. She didn't believe it at first, but it was confirmed, so she was trying to not only learn to deal with the fact that her husband wanted out of their marriage because of another woman, but she was also trying to deal with the fact that her friend betrayed her.

At the same time, she did admit that the marriage had suffered greatly because of her career and that the intimacy she had once felt with her husband was gone. She said they no longer communicated as before. From the way she described it, I would say the marriage was basically over when the affair began. I'm not saying that excuses anyone's behavior, but it does shed some light on how these things happen. It makes the vulnerability more understandable.

Especially in a situation such as the one involving Shania and Mutt, you have to wonder, *What the heck was he thinking? She's Shania! She's gorgeous, she's talented, she's intelligent, she's... Shania!* But she wasn't there. She was on the road. She was busy, and their relationship had changed drastically.

When they got together, Shania was a young woman who was dependent upon Mutt. He practically built her career with his own hands. And that's not to take anything away from her. She's really talented, but he's Mutt Lange! She went from a new-comer to

Nashville, with a first album that basically went nowhere, to doing things that hadn't been done before, and being on top, which was largely due to Mutt's co-writing and producing her album *The Woman In Me*. I love that CD.

Shania then became a star and no longer needed her husband in the way she had before her career took off. I'm not saying that's the reason for the affair, but when the dynamics of a relationship change in such dramatic ways, there's always a chance that one or both of the parties involved will not feel the same toward the other. Mutt went from being the star in the relationship, to being 'Shania's husband.' I mean, he's never been the type to crave the spotlight. In fact, he shies away from it. But the fact that she was thrust into the spotlight, becoming such a sensation, also could've contributed to the demise of the relationship.

Another one of those writer friends of mine, Gail, had a similar experience. Imagine you're sitting down to have dinner with your husband and children. The doorbell rings, and you go to answer it. The mailman hands you the mail, and you take it to your husband, who looks through it. When he gets to a particular postcard, he turns it over and reads it as the color leaves his face. He puts the card under his plate to hide it from you, but says nothing about it. After he finishes eating, he apparently forgets about the card, and you retrieve it. You see that it's from one of your best friends. It reads, "Thank God the rabbit didn't die. We are good for another month anyway."

For those of you who are too young to know, she was referring to an 'old-timey' pregnancy test. Injecting the urine of a pregnant woman into a female rabbit would cause its ovaries to change, due to the hormones in the urine. The common misconception was that the rabbit would die only if the woman was pregnant. Thus, the phrase, 'the rabbit died,' became a euphemism for a positive pregnancy test.

Anyway, when Gail saw the postcard, naturally, she was livid. Not only had her husband cheated on her, but one of her best friends had also betrayed her. The woman had babysat her children, and they had hung out together and even played cards in her home, with her husband! When Gail found out, she confronted him. He told her, "It all started when she bent over to get something out of the oven." The nerve!

Gail called the woman and told her, "I know. I got the card. I have nothing to forgive you for. You've spurred me to take the action I already knew I needed to take."

Now, that's what I'm talking about! Gail handled herself with dignity. She let the woman know she knew, but she didn't attack her. And by not blaming her, Gail was able to focus on the fact that her husband was the one who cheated on her, and then leave and move on. Granted, the so-called friend also betrayed her, but that friend hadn't made a vow before God not to. Know what I mean? I'm pretty sure that woman was also in Gail's rear-view mirror.

There are always many dynamics that make up a relationship, not to mention our personalities and everything that makes us who we are. Sometimes the things that once felt good to us are no longer desirable or even comfortable to us. And sometimes the things you need are things you no longer find in your partner, but do find in someone else. These are all things that make us human, and thus, imperfect.

Every case of infidelity is humiliating, difficult, and painful. But in the situations in which the other woman is someone close to the betrayed, the pain is multiplied many times over. This ultimate betrayal makes the prospect of trusting *anyone* much more difficult than it would be for someone who had been betrayed by a partner who was with a stranger.

Contacting the Other Woman

I haven't ever done that. Contacting the other woman takes a lot of courage and strength, and a willingness to deal with whatever you find out. But if she were a friend or family member, or even an acquaintance, I would've had to. I never really knew. At least, I don't think I did. But you never can be sure.

First of all, I'm going to ask that you don't flip out and go all ghetto or mafia on her. No drive-bys. No firearms. No knives. No brass knuckles. No weapons of any kind. No name-calling. Remember yourself. Keep your dignity. If you go to her or call her and go off on her, you won't be able to believe anything she says. She would probably make things up, even if she wasn't seeing your man, just to put you in your place. So be cool.

Be nice. Approach her as one woman trying to get information from another woman in a friendly manner. Ask questions without an accusatory tone. Make her trust you. Tell her you don't want to upset her or to cause trouble, but you're trying to find the truth about something you feel in your gut… or something like that.

The truth is that unless she's married or in another relationship, she wants you to know. Being a secret is degrading. She wants to tell you, but your man might've sworn her to secrecy. If she's denying it, but you're picking up on the fact that she's lying, tell her you don't mean to offend her, but you feel like there might be something she's not telling you. Tell her that your man has been lying to you, and you're afraid that he's probably lying to her, too. That'll get her attention. She wants to know what's going on between you and him, because nine times out of ten, he's telling her that there's no relationship between the two of you.

Give her some information. Tell her you know he's probably trying to make you out to be a bad person and that you figure he's telling her that he doesn't love you anymore, but it's just not true. Tell her about the backrub he gave you last night before you made love. Tell her about the earrings he gave you for Christmas. You'll be able to tell from her reaction, whether or not it bothers her. And if she's not involved with him, why would it bother her?

She might get upset enough, when she realizes that he's been lying to her about you, that she could open up and tell you everything. Yeah, that's going to sting like salt in a paper cut, but you need to know the truth. And she's much more likely to give it to you than he is. You need to deal with reality, and you have a very slim chance of getting the truth from him.

There's always the possibility that she could lie, too. But she has a lot less reasons to lie than he does. The thing she is most inclined to lie about is whether or not he loves her—how close they are. She doesn't want you to think that he's using her. She wants to be validated, and telling you that he said he loves you, instead of her, would be validation for *you*. But as far as the facts of the relationship (if there really is one), she'll probably be glad to tell you, because truth be known, she's hoping you'll divorce him.

However, as you'll see in the next part of the book, in some states, the other woman or other man can be sued by the spouse of the cheater. In those states, if she knows about the laws, she's not going to admit anything for fear of being sued.

If you do talk to her, you should prepare to feel like you've had your heart ripped right out of your chest. But I'd rather face the facts and deal with the pain than to have that constant gnawing, wondering if what I believe is true. That hurts, too. And remember this: She's not your enemy. She's hurting, too.

I'm not going to say that you *should* contact the other woman. You have to swallow your pride to ask another woman if she's sleeping with your partner. But I think that if I had a suspicion of whom she was, I'd probably have to contact her, especially if my man were denying anything was going on after I had found enough evidence to warrant my concern. Only you can decide if that's the best move for you, but I would want to hear it from her.

Can I Sue Her?

This goes back to blaming the other woman and punishing her, rather than the married cheater. That makes about as much sense to me as aiming the water hoses at the house next door to the one that's burning.

Believe it or not, there are seven states—Illinois, Mississippi, New Hampshire, New Mexico, South Dakota, Utah, and North Carolina— which still have two ancient laws on their books called Alienation of Affection and Criminal Conversation. The other 43 states abolished the laws, which originated in England in the 1800s.

Criminal Conversation is not what it sounds like. They won't arrest you for talking to someone, but it's almost that ridiculous. It's a law that allows the betrayed spouse to sue the other woman or man.

In order to sue, the plaintiff has to prove the following:

* An act of intercourse,

* The existence of a valid marriage between the plaintiff and the adulterous spouse,

* The bringing of the lawsuit within the applicable statute of limitations.

The only possible defense would be proof that the plaintiff consented to the sexual relationship before it took place or proof that the separation was intended to be permanent. How do you prove that?

North Carolina, for example, requires a period of separation of one full year before married couples can file for divorce! During that year, if either spouse has sex with anyone else, that person (the other woman or man) can be sued by the spouse!

And get this! THE OTHER MAN OR WOMAN CAN BE SUED EVEN IF HE OR SHE WERE *NOT AWARE* THAT THE PERSON WITH WHOM HE OR SHE WAS INVOLVED WAS MARRIED! That alone speaks to the absurdity of the law!

Alienation of Affection is another law that allows the betrayed spouse to sue the other man or woman. To succeed, the spouse does not have to prove extramarital sex.

The proof needed to file this lawsuit is as follows:

* The marriage entailed love between the spouses in some degree,

* The spousal love was alienated and destroyed,

* The defendant's malicious conduct contributed to or caused the loss of affection.

The plaintiff does *not* have to prove that the defendant intended to break up the marriage—only that he or she intentionally did things that would affect the marriage. Unlike Criminal Conversation, if the other man or woman is not aware of the fact that the person with whom he or she is involved is married, that *is* a defense against a case of Alienation of Affection. If the defendant was not the pursuer, the plaintiff might not be able to prove intentional or malicious action, which could be a defense.

Supporters of these laws contend that they are an effective way to protect the institution of marriage by punishing the "non-spouse wrong-doer" by ordering monetary compensation to be paid to the spouse of the cheater.

So for clarity, I'll reiterate that these laws provide the right of the wife of a cheater to sue the other woman for having sex with her husband and for causing him to stop loving her. WHAT'S WRONG WITH THIS PICTURE? The cheater is not punished in these scenarios! The person he cheated with, who might not have even known he was married, is punished!

In the divorce proceedings, the judge might award the betrayed spouse a higher settlement, but in some states, that is limited by the equitable distribution law. So the cheater wreaks havoc all around, causing another person to be sued for his infidelity, and he walks away with a slap on the wrist, if that. This makes no sense! If these people are concerned about protecting the sanctity of marriage, why are they not punishing the cheater—the one who is in the marriage and damaging it?

In a letter from a visitor to my *Cheaters & Broken Hearts* website, a man who lived in one of the states mentioned above told me that his other woman had been sued and had to pay his former spouse almost $30,000! He said that it didn't affect him at all, but he hated the fact that the other woman had been punished for something he did. I agree.

If you live in one of the states with those archaic laws, you'd better be extremely careful about the person with whom you get involved, because if you aren't, you might end up in court!

It's obvious that I'm angry about these laws. You might be wondering if I were sued. No, I wasn't sued. But I can't believe that people actually think these are fair laws. They are senseless, and they need to be taken off the books.

The Love Factor

When you're reeling from the hell of infidelity, you want to blame someone, and you want to make it as ugly as possible in your mind and in the minds of others. You immediately think of the cheater as a monster and the other woman as… well, a bigger monster. But what about love?

We've been taught to believe that men only cheat for one reason—sex. That's usually the case, but not always. In some instances of infidelity, you have to consider the love factor. Sometimes it is about a need for emotional intimacy—love.

I know that love is hard to reconcile with the idea of the two monsters getting together with nothing on their minds but jumping into bed, only to destroy the lives of you and your children. But the truth is that many cheating couples, especially those with unfinished business from the past, are actually in love. They might be married to other people, but the feelings are still there. A chance meeting, in a situation like that, can turn into a realization of those feelings.

You're saying that it's still wrong. Correct. You say that if they have to be together, they should first get divorced or out of their current relationships. And you're right about that, too. In a perfect world, that's how it would be handled. On second thought, in a perfect world, that would never happen. But in most cases, they never meant for it to happen. They weren't looking for each other. They were just coincidentally in the same place at the same time.

Eyes meet, sparks fly, and the rest is history. When you feel that instant chemistry with someone you don't know, you can remind yourself that this is a stranger and that you can't jeopardize your relationship by getting involved with someone who could turn out to be a nutcase. But if you know her, and you know she is a good-hearted person with whom you have good memories and residual feelings, it's not so easy to say 'no' to just a drink.

But then 'just a drink' turns into dinner, and dinner turns into a few more drinks, and the next thing you know, it's a done deal. Neither was looking for each other, or anyone else, for that matter. It's just one of those things. That's not to say it's right or even okay. It's not. But they begin to wonder if it's meant to be.

But it could be a test. And if you're in a good relationship with someone who is good to you—someone you love—you would have to think that it's a test. But what if you're in an unhappy relationship? It would be a lot easier to think that it was part of a much bigger plan, and therefore, fate, especially in a situation where the odds were astronomically against your ever having any contact again. Yet there you are.

If you are the one who was betrayed, that's not what you want to hear. But look at it this way: If it were meant to be with the cheating couple, then you know what you had wasn't what you thought it was. And if he still loved and wanted a woman from his past, would you still want to be with him?

In my opinion, if a man loves another woman and wants to be with her, his partner would be much better off without him. It hurts to realize that and to face it, but you can choose to see it as a positive thing. You're now free to find someone who loves and wants to be with you. Sometimes tragedies are blessings in disguise.

Should I Stay, or Should I Go?

One of the first things you try to figure out when you find that your man has been cheating on you is whether you should stay with him or not. I'm not a therapist, but even a therapist won't come out and tell you what you should do. What they (and I) try to do is to get you to look at the facts and the issues and then come to your own conclusions.

However, sometimes, especially when you're in the midst of a crisis, it's hard to see those facts and issues. Your emotions are overwhelming, and you can't even face the facts, not to mention deal with the issues. I'm going to give you a list of steps to help you figure out whether you should stay or go.

Stop the carnage!
The first thing you should do is try to stop the carnage. Step out of panic mode and tone it down a few notches. Give yourself some time to calm down and think. That's not easy, because you want to do something to make yourself feel better, or make him feel worse, but that's not in your best interest if you just found out.

Consider my own feelings.
The next thing you should do is think about your own feelings. What exactly is it that you're feeling? You're hurt, angry, and embarrassed,

just to name a few. But *why* do you feel that way? Do you really love him, or are you just afraid to be alone? Is it that *I don't want him, but I don't want you to have him, either* thing? Or are you just angry because you can't believe he would have the nerve to be with another woman?

Sometimes it's hard to figure out whether you love someone, or if you're just co-dependent. The lines get blurry. For that reason, I recommend that you read **Women Who Love Too Much** by Robin Norwood. It's an excellent book that can help you figure out what you're doing and why you're doing it.

Does he love me?

If you think you love him, the next thing to figure out is whether or not he loves you. That's a tough one. He might say he does one day and say he doesn't the next. If so, I'd say that the writing is on the wall. In other words, if he doesn't know from one day to the next whether he loves you or not, he probably doesn't, and he just doesn't want to tell you. It's difficult to tell someone you don't love her. If he says he loves you, but he doesn't act like he does, trust his actions. And if he doesn't love you, as I said before, you're better off without him. I mean, you don't really want to be with a man who doesn't love you. Do you? I know I don't.

Can I trust him?

Let's say that you do love him, and he's convincing you that he also loves you. He says he's willing to put the other woman out of his life, having no more contact with her at all. Can you trust him? *Should* you trust him? If he gets annoyed when you ask where he's been, or if he has a problem giving you his email and social media passwords, then you probably should not trust him. If he hides his phone from you, or if he leaves the room to take calls, you definitely shouldn't trust him. And if you can't trust him, do you really want to be with him? (Refer back to **How Do I Know He's Cheating?** in Chapter 2.)

Consider who he is.

What if you love him, and you think you can trust him, or at least, you're willing to give it a try? Look at the kind of person he is. Is this just another piece of your heart that he's torn out by cheating again? Is he a drug addict and/or alcoholic? Is he immature, still having to go

73

out at night "with the guys," which usually means hooking up with women? And most importantly, is he abusive in any way? If you answered 'yes' to any of those things, STOP! Immaturity is the only one of those things that might get better as he gets older, unless he gets professional help. In the meantime, do you want to deal with those things? I hope not! None of them should be tolerated.

Does he want out?

If he wants a divorce or a break-up, give it to him! Nothing good can ever come from holding onto a man who wants to get away from you! Trying to hold onto him will only make him angry and resentful, and that won't help anyone. Let him go, even if you think it will kill you. It won't. Trust me. If it would, women would be dropping like flies.

Does he want to stay?

What if he wants to make it work? Was it just a one-time thing? Is this the first time he's cheated in a long relationship where he has otherwise treated you with love and respect? Is he normally an honest person? Does he take care of you and your children? Is he a good father? Does he feel remorseful? Is he willing to do whatever it takes to make your relationship work? If you answered 'yes' to these questions (or most of them), maybe you should give the man another chance. Especially if he treats you with love and respect, he might be worth holding on to. I'm not saying you should trust him after the infidelity. Trust is something he should be willing to work to rebuild. But maybe you should deliberate about giving it another try… taking baby steps. If you've been out of the dating world for a long time, you can't imagine how awful it is, so chew on that, too.

What's best for the children?

I know that all your life, you've had it drilled into your head that it's ALWAYS better to 'stay together for the kids.' That's all well and good if you can have a decent relationship without a lot of tension, where the children can be happy and feel secure. However, if you and your man are either not speaking to each other or arguing about where he was, who he was with, what time he got home, etc., you are NOT doing those children any favors by being together. You can do way more harm than good, not only to your children, but also to yourself, if you choose to stay in a relationship that's already broken!

In staying with a man who doesn't love and respect you enough to be faithful to you, you're teaching your boys to disrespect women and that cheating is okay. You're also teaching your daughters to look the other way and to not respect themselves enough to expect a man to be faithful to them. In essence, you're teaching your children to have the same kind of relationship you have with your man. I'm sure you don't want that for them.

As Dr. Phil says, "It's better to be *from* a broken home than to be *in* one." I agree. I'm from a 'broken home,' but it was broken long before they divorced. I literally begged my mother to leave my father. There was no physical abuse, and the arguments were not constant, but the tension was. You could cut it with a knife. It was uncomfortable, at best. I spent most of my childhood in my bedroom, avoiding my family. We would've all been much better off if they had divorced when I was a young child.

Can I forgive him?
Do you think you can forgive him? This one is really important. And it's more important for you than it is for him. Regardless of what happens between you and him, forgiving him sets your heart free. It allows you to let go of the pain and go on with your life, whether it's with him or without him. But if you choose to stay with him, and you're not able to forgive him, it won't ever work. Forgiveness is essential. (See *Unforgiveness Is a Cancer* in Chapter 6.)

What about my self-esteem?
How would staying with him affect your self-esteem? Could you respect yourself if you stay with him? Sometimes it's hard to know at first. This one might take a while to realize. Don't confuse pride and ego with self-respect. Pride is not good, but self-respect is necessary. If you feel ashamed or that you're stupid or crazy for being with him, maybe you should pay attention to those feelings. That's not to say that you *are* stupid or crazy—you're not. But those feelings could be telling you something. Maybe your heart is tired of being his punching bag.

Should I get counseling?
Yes, yes, and yes. As you know, I suggest that anyone faced with this crisis get some counseling. The decision to leave a relationship or not,

and especially a marriage, can have life-altering effects for many people. Making that decision while your heart is shattered into a million pieces is not advised. Talking with a therapist can help you to sort through the issues, try to put the pieces back together, and figure out what's best for you.

Do I need legal advice?

Absolutely! If you're married or living together, consulting with an attorney is extremely important! If you're thinking that you do want to end your marriage, don't do anything until you speak with an attorney. Making moves prematurely can be costly, so don't make that mistake.

Deciding what to do when you find that your man has cheated is a difficult thing to do. There's no way to know for sure what another person is feeling or thinking, or what they're going to do. That's why you have to focus on *your* feelings and what's best for *you*.

I cannot stress this point enough: *YOU CANNOT MAKE THIS DECISION BASED UPON WHAT HE WANTS OR WHAT YOU THINK IS BEST FOR HIM.* He obviously wants to have his cake and eat it, too. You can't allow him to have that. Love yourself enough to make the choice that's good for you.

People, especially women, tend to fear the unknown. After being with a man for a long time, you can't imagine life without him. However, when he does things to cause you pain, and possibly cause you to become depressed, you have to accept the fact that you need to make changes in your life before things will get better. It might be scary, but when you compare it to the thought of living the rest of your life with a cheater, it's not so bad.

If you still love him, it's going to hurt like crazy if you decide to let him go, but that doesn't mean you should go back. In most cases, being away from him won't hurt nearly as much as staying with him, once you get through that adjustment period!

And if you're the other woman, you should NEVER stay with the cheater. Remember, he's cheating on you, too. He's disrespecting you by being with you while he's committed to someone else.

Leaving an unfaithful partner hurts, but that pain will heal. Staying with an unfaithful partner is a guarantee that pain and depression will always be a part of your life.

Trying to Bring Him Back

You're doing *whaaaaat*? That man left you for another woman, and you what? You want him back? What are you thinking? Stop it!

Just chill on this and think about it. First of all, why would you want to be with a man who would treat you that way? Do you think it would be different if he came back? Even if he wanted to come back, which he doesn't if he hasn't, he would still be cheating on you. If he cared enough about her to leave you for her, he would more than likely leave you for her again. I wouldn't bet the farm on it, but it's almost a given. And if he didn't leave you for *her*, he might leave you for a different woman.

You have to face the reality that he's not your man. Even if he's your husband, he's not your man. He's going to do what he wants to do, and apparently, he wants to be with her. If you'll think about that, you'll realize that you don't want *him*—the man he really is. You want the man you *thought* he was, or maybe the one he *used to* be. Or maybe the man you *want* him to be. Sweetheart, that guy doesn't exist.

Okay, you've invested years of your life, maybe even a lot of money, you have children together, you own property together, and it's complicated…. I get it. But the bottom line is that you can't make someone love you or want you. And you need to love yourself and respect yourself enough to do what's best for you, which is to let him go! You can't force him to be with you, but even if you could, you wouldn't be happy with that. You'd live in constant fear that he was going to leave you again. And every time he walked out the door, you'd be afraid he was going to be with her.

You're lonely—hug your dog. You're horny—get a vibrator. You miss talking to him—talk to someone else. When you're missing him so desperately that you're almost ready to drive over to her house and drag him out, kicking and screaming, sit down and write out a list of all the things you don't like about him and the things he's done to hurt you. Keep that sucker with you 24/7, and when you get weak, pull it out and read it again… and again… and again. Focus on all the pain he's caused you until your mind is able to overpower your heart, and your desire to bring back the source of your agony subsides.

So you say you're not really trying to get him back, but you're just waiting in case he wants to come back. See above! Girlfriend, if you let him come back, he might do that someday… temporarily. I know a guy who left his wife for another woman. It didn't work out for him with that woman, so his wife let him move back in. He stayed there until he found another place to live and another woman, and then he was gone. Letting him come back and then having him leave again was like ripping the scab off a healing wound. All she did was open herself up to be hurt by him once more. That was the worst possible thing she could've done, short of suicide or homicide.

Don't be his safety net. Don't be his security blanket. If he has the nerve to show up at your door, don't tell yourself you'll sleep with him 'just this once for old times' sake.' If you do, your heart and mind will get all tangled up with the memories of the sex, and you'll be back to square one. Kick his sorry butt to the curb, where he belongs!

I Don't Want Him, But…

You know what I'm talking about. "I don't want him, but I don't want you to have him, either."

You can't stand the sight of him because of what he's done to you, but the thought of her having him makes you feel like you're going to lose your lunch. You're not even sure you love him anymore, but it tears you up inside to know that he wants someone else. You guessed it. I've been there, too. It's hard to admit that one, but I held onto an abusive, cheating guy for about three years, because I couldn't stand the thought of seeing him with his ex. I was sure he'd go back to her… but he didn't. It wasn't easy seeing him with other women, but once I got past the adjustment and grieving period, it was a lot easier than being with him.

It's human nature. It's almost like a competition. Even when you know someone is bad for you, and you don't even really want him anymore, you don't want to let go and allow him to be with someone else. It's like that little girl who's had a toy for a while and got tired of it, and she doesn't want to play with it anymore, but she panics when she sees another child playing it. "You can't have that! It's mine! Give it back!"

Yeah, it really does hurt to think that a guy you think of as belonging to you could want to be with someone else, especially if he leaves you for her. But don't let that stand in the way of logical thinking. Yes, it's natural to want to hold onto someone you think of as yours, but is it wise? Would you want to hold onto him if he were a child molester or a murderer? Probably not. So why do you want to keep your cheater?

Think about what he's doing to you and the way he's hurting you. Keep in mind how selfish he is, being with her, knowing how much he's hurting you. He knew you would be devastated if you found out, but he chose to be with someone else anyway. And regardless of what he says, he would do it again, especially if he shows no remorse.

So why is it that you want to hold onto him? Because he's yours? Apparently, he isn't. Because it's going to hurt like hell to know he's with her? I know. It will. But aren't you already in agony? Trust me on this. The pain you'll feel in knowing he's with someone else will fade. You'll get over it. But if you stay with a man who cheats on you, that awful feeling will be with you for as long as you're with him.

You don't want her to have him? You don't want her to be happy with him? Don't worry. There's a pretty good chance he'll do to her what he's doing to you. It's not guaranteed, but it's likely. And even if he doesn't, it won't be smooth sailing. You might not realize this, but whether she admits it or not, she's jealous of you. She might not even admit it to herself, but she wishes she had been with him all that time. She wishes she had borne his children. She panics when he's in your house to see your children, to get some things, or to give you some money. She looks at your children, and she sees you, and she thinks of the two of you together, making those children, and the closeness and happiness you had at their births, and the way the two of you worked together to be a family.

I know you're hurting. She probably won't ever admit it, but she's hurting, too. And so is he. But if he wants to be with her, let him go.

Don't think of him as your toy that another little girl is playing with. Maybe he's her toy now. And maybe he'll be someone else's toy someday. But if you have to think of him that way, think of him as a *broken* toy. It doesn't work anymore, and pieces are missing. It's not fun to play with anymore. You had some good times with it, but since it's broken, those times are over. It's time to throw it away.

Going Out With "The Guys"

When he says he's going out with "the guys," we are usually afraid that he's looking for another woman. But what if it's not a woman he's interested in? You might think you would know if he were gay. But maybe he isn't gay. Maybe he's bisexual. You think you'd still know? Did you know that lots of professional football players are gay? Don't be fooled by the stereotype. There are some who seem like the manliest of men, but they like it both ways.

Does he have a special guy friend he hangs out with all the time? Is he on the phone with him more than he is with you? Does he smile a lot when he's on the phone with him? Does he talk about him all the time?

Okay, those things don't necessarily mean that he's having a gay affair, but it does happen. I have a friend who is a private investigator, and he says that it's happening more and more all the time. Usually, a woman calls him because she's afraid her husband has another woman. But he said that he's actually followed men into adult book stores and caught them in booths with other men. And these are married men.

My friend also told me about a woman who was suspicious of her husband because she had seen that he had been on a website called RouletteChat. It's a social network where people go on and do video chats with other people. The woman wanted video evidence of her husband… uh, *pleasuring himself* on that site. My friend didn't give her what she wanted, because he found the process of finding that proof revolting.

Though it's still vastly more probable that if your man is cheating, it's with a woman, there is that chance he's taking a walk on an even wilder side than you thought. Just because he's hanging out with a guy doesn't mean he isn't cheating.

Advice for the Betrayed

Everyone who has ever had the experience of having a partner cheat knows the way it feels—kind of like an earthquake! It seems that everything you ever knew as being stable is now shaken and crumbling out from under you. It's almost like a sensation of falling, because everything seems so out of control, and you don't know what's going to happen, what you're going to do, or where you're going to land.

That's why it's important to take some time to let the earth stop shaking. Get your footing and try to calm down. This might take a few hours, a few days, or even a few months. But before you start making decisions you might regret (like pulling the children out of school to move back to your parents' home in Florida), you need to get to where you can think clearly and see things for what they really are.

At first, you might imagine that your man is planning to leave to be with his other woman, and at that point, you might be ready to toss him out! But after thinking about things, analyzing the details, and understanding how he feels and what he wants, you might want to reconsider the tossing plan.

As I said before, if he is a decent man who made a mistake, he regrets it, and he's willing to spend the rest of his life making it up to you, think about that. Is his mistake worth giving up everything you've shared together? Only you can make that decision.

There is no shame in getting a therapist's help for anything, but definitely not for something as painful as infidelity. It changes your sense of self, and of your world. Trying to cope with this type of experience without help is like walking through a forest blindfolded. You won't ever find your way out. Talking to friends and family is fine, but they are biased. You need to talk to someone who is unbiased.

However, regardless of what you plan to do, do not allow yourself to believe the world is coming to an end. It feels like it, but it's not. If it does end, it won't be because of a cheater! If infidelity would cause the world to end, it would've been over a long, long time ago.

I know that some of you are having suicidal thoughts. Up until a few years ago, I thought everyone had them. When I found out that everyone didn't, that's when I realized how severe my depression and pain had been for most of my life. I knew it was horrible, but I assumed that everyone had unbearable pain and thought about suicide.

I've been blessed with the fear of going to Hell. That might not sound like a blessing, but it is for me. Even though I am a Christian, that fear, and my desire to not hurt those I love, has kept me alive. Well, that and therapy. And I'm glad to be alive! If I had taken my life the first time I had suicidal thoughts, I wouldn't have made it past my mid teens, and it makes me sad to think of the wonderful times I would've missed if I had acted on those urges. And if I had killed myself back then, I would've deprived the world of a very special person—my daughter! That would be a terrible shame.

Think about that old saying, "It's darkest before the dawn." I hold onto that, because it's true. There have been times when I thought there was no way my life could get better. It seemed that only darkness was ahead. I had no hope. But because of my fear and my love for my daughter, I held on. Now, I'm so thankful that I did, because even though things are far from perfect for me, I have good times. I love. I laugh. I enjoy things. I've accomplished things. I'm still accomplishing things—writing books! I can do positive things with my life that, in those dark hours of my despair, I couldn't ever imagine happening. You can, too.

If you're having suicidal thoughts, call a crisis line NOW! Do not wait! If you can't find a crisis line, call 911. And if you're taking pills and drinking, call 911. You might not think you've taken enough to kill you, but you might not wake up in the morning. It's not worth the risk. You don't really want to die. Make the call!

In my first marriage, I called a crisis line once. I felt completely hopeless. I was sitting on the couch with my .357 Magnum in one hand and a bottle of wine in the other. I had decided that I couldn't take any more pain. I was trying to determine whether I should shoot him when he came in, or to shoot myself and be done with it. I knew I didn't really want to die. I just wanted the agony to stop. And I didn't want to spend the rest of my life in prison for killing him.

I found the phone book. I called Safe Place, which is a shelter for battered women. I left home and spent the night there. The women at the shelter set me up with a therapist, and that was the beginning of my realization that I didn't have to live that way. It took a while, but I finally gained the strength to leave. It wasn't easy, but I did it. And you can do it, too.

Okay, after you get past that crisis point, and you're in the midst of trying to figure out how you're going to change your life for the better, don't forget about taking care of yourself. I'm not suggesting that you should run twelve miles if you aren't used to exercising… or even if you are used to it. Just get up. Move around. Put on some makeup. Style your hair. We all feel better when we look better.

Hug your children—the humans and the furry ones. Tell them how much you love them. Get out and visit some people. I know it's hard to do that when you're feeling so bad, but being around people who care for you reminds you that your life is NOT as hopeless as it feels right now. And even in that agonizing state, there are people who can make you smile or maybe laugh!

Go to a salon. Have your hair and nails done. Go shopping. Don't buy out the store, but get a new outfit. Even a new shirt or pair of shoes will make you feel better. Go for a walk. Go see a movie. Have lunch with friends. Or maybe go to a nursing home and visit strangers! I know, that sounds depressing, but if you can bring a smile to another person's face, it'll lift your spirits. It'll also make you see that if those people can smile, surely you can get through this and be happy.

Pray. What you can't do for yourself, He can do for you.

There is hope, and there is healing, and that's why you're reading this book. You'll get there.

Chapter 5

The Other Woman

Of the three parties involved in a love triangle, I think the other woman is the most misunderstood and, more importantly, the most blamed and hated. I'm sure the other man also gets a lot of rage directed toward him from the man his lover betrayed, but I don't ever remember hearing the 'other man' blamed when a woman cheats on her husband.

Oh, I take that back. A friend of mine sort of blamed his wife's lover for her affair. As you might've guessed, my friend was still with his cheating wife. If he wasn't still with her, I'm fairly confident that he would be blaming his wife, rather than the man she cheated with. But that's one—ever.

Maybe the reason people are so quick to blame the other woman is because of her stereotype. You know what I mean. Everyone thinks of her as being the super-hot, irresistible, gorgeous woman with huge breasts, who lounges around, day and night, wearing a teddy, high heels, and lots of makeup. She lurks, lying in wait for an innocent, unsuspecting family man who has no interest in her. She forces herself upon him and seduces him 'against his will.' After she's had her way with him, he quickly flees from her, feeling violated, and immediately reports the rape to the authorities. Absolutely absurd, right?

Oh, and the bunny boiler in *Fatal Attraction*! That's a good movie. I'll admit, I've seen it many times. Great actors, great suspense... But it really bothers me, because it perpetuates the stereotype of the psycho other woman. Women, 'mistress' or otherwise, do not go around pouring acid on cars, kidnapping children, and trying to kill people. Granted, those things have happened, but they're exceedingly rare. There's a much greater chance of a man doing things like that than a woman doing them.

Okay, there probably have been a lot of cars or trucks 'keyed' by jilted women. I would imagine there have also been quite a few tires punctured by women in jealous rages. But as a rule, a heart-broken woman plots revenge in her fantasies, and that's usually about as far as it goes.

So how *do* you see her? How different is your idea of the other woman? You probably think of her as being beautiful, with a great body. She's crazy hot. She's evil and selfish, never caring about anyone or anything but herself. Can you deny buying into that stereotype?

The truth is that the other woman is just that—another woman. She might be beautiful, but she might also be ordinary. She could be sexy, but not necessarily sexier than you or any other woman. She might wear a teddy and heels, or she might wear sweats and running shoes. She might pursue your man, but just as likely, or even more so, he pursued her. She's not a monster... she's just a woman. And she's hurting, too.

The other woman usually has low self-esteem and has trouble finding a mate. Regardless of whether or not she's aware that he's married, she's just happy to have someone show her some affection.

She probably had a father who was either absent or emotionally unavailable to her. She's subconsciously drawn to men she can't have and/or men who aren't capable of loving her. Also subconsciously, that type of man (unavailable) is instinctively drawn to her.

The other woman is like any woman—she wants love and security. The problem is that she doesn't know how to find those things. She knows that she won't find what she needs in a man who is married or in a serious relationship, but he's there, and he wants her, so she gives in to him.

Another myth about the other woman is that she's happy in her relationship with another woman's man. She has moments of happiness when she's with him. But even then, she's dreading when he leaves, knowing he's going home to be with his wife. She usually falls hard and fast for him and suffers deeply during the relationship, and in some cases, for years afterward.

In the eyes of the other woman, the cheaters' wife is the one who has it all. She gets the nights, the holidays, his name, his children, his home, his love.... All the other woman gets is a few stolen minutes, or hours, if she's lucky. She has a lot of time alone to drink herself into oblivion while she watches her phone, hoping for a call or text from him, and grieves over the fact that the man she loves is at home with his family—not with her.

However, there are a few women who seem like mutants to me. No, actually, they seem more like men. They can have sex indiscriminantly, separating sex from emotion, and take advantage of whatever a man is willing to give them, while going on with their lives, unaffected. Those are the exceptions—not the rule. They do exist, but they are not representative of the other woman or of women in general.

In case you hadn't noticed, men have a tendency to be dishonest if that's what it takes to get what they want. (Sorry, guys, but I've even had men tell me that—not to mention my own experiences with them.) Often, the cheater tells the other woman he is single or divorced. She has no idea he has a family at home. She usually becomes suspicious, but by the time she finds out, she's head over heels in love with him. She can't let go, and he gets to continue to have it all.

Another reason I believe so many women blame the other women when their men cheat is because *the cheater blames the other woman*! How convenient! Also, extremely cowardly! The betrayed woman loves him and wants to hold onto him, so rather than placing the blame where it should be, on the cheater, she directs all her rage toward the other victim in the triangle—the woman she sees as her adversary.

I know what you're thinking: *She should've stopped and considered his wife and children!* The way I see it, HE should've stopped and considered his wife and children! Again, you have to remember that she might not even know about them. Even if she does, he's told her lots of different reasons why he's cheating on her and why he's getting a divorce. It doesn't have to be true. It just has to sound good. And when you're in love with a guy, you want to believe him, so you do.

Being the other woman can be, and usually is, just as agonizing as being the cheater's partner. That's because when a woman is in love with a man who is married, or in a committed relationship with someone else, it's as if the other woman is constantly condoning his cheating on her on a daily basis. That destroys what little self-esteem she might've had going into the relationship. She craves validation of her love, but she rarely ever gets it. That's because most cheating men who do leave, even if they divorce their wives, do NOT stay with the women with whom they cheated.

Carla, another friend of mine, is involved with a guy she dated briefly in high school. They met on Facebook, and after a few months of casual communication, she started seeing him.

She says she's happy with him but that nights are difficult. And holidays are really painful. But his wedding anniversary is her most dreaded day. She says she knows the relationship will possibly end someday, but she'll just have to deal with that when it happens. It seems to me that she's refusing to think about it, ignoring the elephant in the room sort of thing.

She said the most excruciating thing she had to deal with in her relationship with him was when he was in the hospital. He had fallen on the ice and hit his head. He texted her from the hospital, saying something about the ER. She was in a panic, but she couldn't go to see him or even call him. She had no rights. As far as the world was concerned, she was nobody to him. And she knew that if he hadn't been able to text or call her, no one would've notified her, because to those close to him, she didn't exist. She sat in the hospital parking lot and cried for hours. He called and texted her, even with his wife and mother in the room, but that experience highlighted the fact that the woman by his side was his wife, and Carla was his woman on the side.

He's offered to move away with her, but she knows she would be blamed for his being away from his family. Carla would be the bad guy. She says she knows there's no way for her to win in that situation, but she just can't say 'good-bye' to him.

When a woman is involved with a married man, and he leaves his wife, the other woman sees it as validation of her and of their relationship. She assumes he will marry her, but she is usually either cast aside or finds herself to be one of several that he's seeing. After years of marriage, the last thing he wants is to get married again. He sees himself as being free, and he wants to take full advantage of that. Even if he cares for his other woman, he wants to experience his freedom and play the field like a teen. Not all men go that route, but most do.

It's at that point, after feeling miserable and worthless, then feeling some hope, only to have it all crash and burn, the woman hits rock bottom. She has to make a decision. Either she's willing to degrade herself even more than she was before by being one of his many playthings, with no self-esteem at all, or she has to end the relationship. Some women find those choices so overwhelmingly painful that suicide seems a better option, which it NEVER is. Though sadly, some choose to end their lives, others turn to drugs and alcohol to numb the pain.

So, you see, you might want her to suffer for being with your man, but you have nothing to worry about. Her suffering is immeasurable.

The Other Man

I believe that a man's experiences as the 'other' are different from a woman's. All of their sexual encounters or relationships are different. They don't see things the way women do. They feel (or don't feel) things in other ways.

Men usually tend to focus more on the physical aspect of the relationship, whereas women are generally more emotional. Therefore, in most cases, a man's experience as being the 'other' is not as painful and traumatic as that of the other woman.

That's not to say that the other man doesn't fall in love or get hurt sometimes by a cheating woman. I'm sure it happens, but most men are much more analytical when it comes to matters of the heart. They are better at building protective walls around their hearts. And they are more prone to be in it just for the sex.

Even if the other man does develop feelings for a cheating woman, the odds are in favor of his ending the relationship, rather than being the tragic figure that so many women become in that situation. He will move on quickly, finding other women to distract him from his pain. He might still carry a torch for that woman, but he's not inclined to be incinerated by it.

How Do I Know He's Married?

Getting involved with an unavailable man is not a good idea. Agreed? Sometimes you actually know the guy, so you know he's married. But what if you just met him? What if he lies?

It would be great if it were as simple as looking to see if he's wearing a ring, but nothing is that simple. If there's no ring, don't assume he's available. Ask questions—lots of questions. Ask if he's been married before, how long he was married, how old he is, when his last relationship other than the marriage was, if he ever cheated on his wife or girlfriends, and that sort of thing. If his answers are vague or don't seem to make sense or fit together with other things he's told you, don't believe him. He might not be married, but he could be in a committed relationship, which is almost as bad for you as being married.

Even if he has a quick answer for everything, it's best to check and make sure. Here's why. I met a guy in a club once. He wasn't wearing a ring, he didn't seem to have a tan line from a ring, he said he'd been divorced "since October," he was living with a male roommate (which I verified), and guess what! A month later, when I was completely in love with him, on the day I was moving to the city where he lived to be with him, I found out that he was moving back in with his wife *that day*! THAT was when I found out he was still married!

Lots of men don't like wearing jewelry, and some can't wear a ring because of the type of work they do—machinists, for example. However, I believe the main reason married men don't wear wedding rings is because they don't want women to know they're married.

The married guy I was involved with when I was a teen gave me a lame excuse for why he didn't wear a ring. He said that he broke that finger years ago, and it swelled, and the ring never fit after that. Please. Like he couldn't have had it resized. He obviously didn't want to look the part of the married man.

Okay, so you meet a guy, and he's not wearing a ring. Look for a tan line and/or indentation where the wedding ring should be. If you see the line, the ring might as well be there. He's married, and he thinks you're stupid enough to buy into whatever garbage he tells you. If he's wearing another ring on that finger, it might be to cover that tan line. Ask him to take it off. If he won't take it off, run!

That tan line helps when you meet a man in person, but lots of people meet online. That's much more difficult, but there are warning signs you can pick up even in an online 'relationship.'

The following is a list of signs you should watch for in order to determine whether or not a guy is married or in a committed relationship, whether you meet him in person or online:

* He doesn't give you his number.
My experience with meeting guys online is that they are quick to offer their phone numbers. If he doesn't give you his number after a few emails, either he's not into you, or he's with someone else.

* He gave you his number, but when you call or text after business hours or on weekends, he doesn't respond.
He's with her.

* He asks for your number, and he calls, but he blocks his number.
He can't take a chance that you might call back or text.

* He calls you only during business hours.
After hours, he's with her.

* He sees you, but only at your house or in your town.
He's afraid of being seen with you by someone who knows him.

* He won't give you his address or the name of the company where he works.
He can't have you show up or send something to him.

* He says he's single, but he won't give you any details about his past, especially 'former' relationships.
He's trying to keep you from putting 2+2 together.

* He says he's divorced, but he won't speak specifically about his ex or children.
He's protecting his family—his current wife and children.

* He won't take you out in public.
The wife or kids could see you with him.

* He drives to your house, but he wants to take your car if you go out.
Someone might recognize his car and see you in it.

* He takes you out, but only to obscure places where he won't know anyone.
He's afraid someone might see you with him.

* He always wants to take you out of town.
See above.

* He won't introduce you to people he speaks to when you're with him in public.
If he doesn't introduce you, he can explain you away much easier.

* He won't take you around his family or friends.
They might tell her.

* He won't let you (or anyone else) take pictures of him, especially with you.
That would be hard to explain if seen by the wrong person.

* He won't let you leave personal items at his place.
She would see them.

Some men work away from home and have to have an apartment or hotel suite in the city where they work. If your guy has that kind of setup, he might take you to that 'home,' but if the wife or other women are ever there, he won't allow you to leave anything there. Ask him if he minds. If he says it's okay, don't assume he's not married or that he's not seeing anyone else. Maybe the wife doesn't ever go there. Or maybe he just hides your things when you leave.

I don't know of a website where you can access public records without paying a fee. However, if you're suspicious that someone you're seeing could be married, it's worth paying for the information, especially in the seven states where the other woman (or other man) can be sued by the betrayed spouse! Those states are: Illinois, Mississippi, New Hampshire, New Mexico, South Dakota, Utah, and North Carolina. (Refer back to *Can I Sue Her?* in Chapter 4.)

There are lots of little clues you can pick up on if you pay close attention. For instance, except for sociopaths, most people won't look you in the eye when they're being deceptive. If he won't look you in the eye, or if he won't give you a straight answer, he's hiding something or lying.

Keep emotional distance between you and anyone new. That means DON'T sleep with him too soon, so you can weigh the evidence somewhat objectively. If you sleep with him, you won't want to see the warning signs that might be flashing right in front of your face. Keep your eyes wide open for those signs, because if you don't, you'll wish you had.

Good Sex Does NOT Equal Love

We women get confused sometimes. Most of us have a hard time separating sex from love, though we know they are two different things. They should go hand-in-hand, but that's not always true, especially for men. In fact, probably half the time, sex has nothing to do with love for them. It's about physical release—feeling good in the man parts.

When we find someone with whom we have a strong sexual chemistry, and the sex is always incredibly exciting, we want to hold onto it. Why wouldn't we? It feels amazing. And if it feels that good, it has to mean that you're soulmates, right? Wrong!

We're subconsciously attracted to people who 'feel' familiar to us. So if you grew up in a home where your father abused your mother, or where your father was not necessarily abusive but was emotionally unavailable, that's the kind of guy you'll be drawn to. Consciously, you'd NEVER pick a guy who reminds you of the pain from your childhood, but in the recesses of your mind, that pain feels 'comfortable' to you on some level, because it's familiar.

The man who respects you too much to try to sleep with you in the first month or two might seem boring, and maybe sort of annoying, but he's the one who is much more likely to be there for you and take care of you, as opposed to using and hurting you. It's not exciting, but it's that thrill that gets you into the kinds of relationships that cause you lots of trouble. If you're from a dysfunctional family, remember this: Excitement = pain. Excitement is overrated!

So when you meet a guy who triggers that part of you that is hurt and in need of healing, beware. When you let him inside you, and he does all the things that send you into orbit, it feels like you've found the perfect man for you. But odds are more in favor of his causing you immeasurable agony. Not always. It's not an exact science. But if you had a particularly painful childhood, and you find a guy who makes you scream with passion from day one, you're in danger of having your heart shattered. DO NOT mistake that great sex for love on his part. To him, and to you, whether you know it or not, it's just good sex.

Advice for the Other Woman

First of all, I'd like to say that I, unlike most of the world, do not blame you for the decision a man makes to cheat on his partner. Well, if you're having an affair with your sister's or your friend's man, I'd say you're equally to blame. But unless it's a case of cheating for love, chances are pretty good that if he weren't cheating with you, he'd be cheating with someone else. That's not something you want to hear, but it's true.

Everyone seems to think that you have this great power to lure or seduce a man away from his wife and family. I know that's nonsense. Your power is no greater than any other woman's. However, if the man you're cheating with gets caught or decides to confess to his partner, that's the angle he'll use to get back into her good graces. You'll be the evil seductress, and he'll be the poor, pitiful 'innocent' victim who just couldn't resist your sexual power over him. He'll throw you under the bus so fast, your head will spin!

He'll accuse you of stalking him, pursuing him, or even blackmailing him to get him to be with you. He'll paint you to be the biggest slut in town, with a long list of lovers and a drawer full of sex toys. He'll leave out the part about buying those toys for you and having you use them on him!

He'll swear he never cared for you and that he's been trying to escape your wiles from day one. He'll say he only wanted to be your friend or that he felt sorry for you and was trying to help you in the beginning, but then he fell victim to your wicked ways.

I said all that to make you understand one thing: YOU CANNOT TRUST HIM! I understand that you want to. I know that you probably believe everything he says. I get it—I've been there. It's not something I'm proud of, but it's why I know what I'm talking about, and it's why I'm writing this book. It's also why I can tell you that probably 90% of what he's telling you is NOT TRUE!

I know how you feel. I keep saying that, but really, I do. You care for him, or maybe you're in love with him, so you have to believe what he says in order to justify what you're doing. He knows this, so he's told you a bunch of sob stories about how his marriage is a joke, that they haven't loved each other or slept together in years, that they're only together for the sake of the children, or because he can't afford to leave. He plays on your sympathy to the point that you actually feel sorry for him. But don't! There might be a morsel of truth in what he's saying, but aside from that, he's lying his cute little butt off!

You might think that because he's helping you financially, he's sincere. Of course, he wouldn't give you money if he didn't love you, right? THINK! That's just one step away from prostitution, and he might even see it that way. Please understand that I'm NOT calling you a hooker! I'm just trying to make you see what's happening. Men have been paying for sex forever, and it didn't stop at your doorstep. I know that's a hard one to swallow, but it's important for you to face the facts. I thought that because a man I was with paid my bills for a couple of years, he was being truthful when he said he intended to marry me. But he wasn't. Just like good sex doesn't equal love, money also doesn't equal love.

He's made promises, he's made plans with you, and maybe he's even met your family or friends. He says he loves you more than he's ever loved anyone. He swears the divorce is in the works and berates you for doubting his love if you try to talk with him about it. Face it, girls. You don't know what he's doing. He might be buying his wife or fiancée a house or working on building his family with her!

You just want someone to love you, but it seems that only the married ones are interested in you. You want to believe there are some decent guys out there, so you buy into his lies. But you need to realize that you deserve better than to be his girl on the side. You deserve better than the crumbs he throws you after he dines with his wife. You should be treated with love and respect, and that's something you will NEVER get with a married man! You're already being fed enough of his lies, so don't add to them by lying to yourself. Keeping you on the side is NOT love and respect, and no amount of sugar can coat that one enough to make it sweet.

So he's nice to you, and he buys expensive things for you. Is that all you want? If so, that's your choice. But I'm saying you should be THE woman in a man's life—not A woman in his life. You deserve to share his name and his home. If he can't or won't give that to you, he's not your guy.

You say he's promising he's going to divorce her and marry you. If that's the case, then tell him to give you a call when the divorce is final! I know, you're afraid he'll find someone else if you do that. Well, if he does, that should tell you something. He didn't love you. And aren't you better off knowing that than wasting your time with him?

I know a woman who was in a relationship with a married man for well over 20 years! He was practically a part of her family, even buying her kids their first cars. It might've been a good financial arrangement for her, but at the same time, by wasting her life with him, she blew any chance of finding a man of her own. Don't be that woman.

Let's say he really is a good guy who's just in a bad situation. Let's say he does love you. If that's true, he should be concerned about your feelings and those of his wife. He should think about the way people will blame you for the demise of his marriage if they find that he was seeing you before his divorce. He should stop procrastinating and being selfish and do the right thing. He should either get a divorce, so he can be with you, or stop seeing you and reconcile with his wife. You shouldn't let him have it both ways. The cake... you know.

I've known too many women who have believed the lies of married men. Sometimes we don't even know they're married until we're hooked, but don't think that's a coincidence. They will say or do whatever it takes to get what they want. But you don't have to give it to them! Don't waste the precious years of your life waiting for a man who is pretending to love you and pretending to divorce his wife. Don't waste your child-bearing years (especially) on someone who WILL NOT be there for you when your youth is gone.

Don't believe in the fairytale. Even if he did leave her, few men who leave their wives for another woman ever marry her. And even if you did end up with him, you'd always be labeled "the slut who stole him away from his family." Is that really something you want? No, you don't. It doesn't feel good. It sucks!

I know you think you love him, but trust me on this. You don't even know him! You think you do, but you don't. He seems perfect when he's with you. That's because you're his escape! When he's with you, he's ignoring all his responsibilities, his problems, his bills, and his issues. You're his drug and his way out of everyday life. You're his toy... his fun. You don't see the way he treats his wife, his children, his parents, and his co-workers. You don't see what a slob he is at home. You don't see how inconsiderate and rude he is. You only see what he wants you to see. You don't know him.

There are a few guys who actually do leave their wives, get divorces, and stay with the women with whom they cheated. But as I said, even in those situations, it's far from perfect. You'd have an ex-wife, child support, alimony, property distribution, their debts and obligations, his family, her family, and their children to deal with. And EVERYONE blames you for his choice to leave. That's not the best way to start out a relationship or marriage, to say the least.

What I want you to take away from all of this is that it's a NO-WIN SITUATION when you're involved with, and in love with, a married or otherwise committed man. While he's playing Santa with his wife, you're home alone. While he's at home at night and on weekends with his wife and children, you're home alone. You don't want to commit to any other relationship, or even going out with friends, because your married guy might be able to sneak away for a few minutes, and you want to be there for him if he can squeeze you into his busy schedule. You know, in between the things that are *important* to him.

RESPECT YOURSELF! Remember, if you don't, no one else will, either. You deserve to be the ONLY woman in a man's life. You deserve to be treated respectfully, with love. If you have self-respect, you won't allow yourself to be treated as if you're a second-class citizen... because you aren't!

Probably my most important bit of advice for you is to get some counseling. Yes, I keep saying it, but that's because it's vital. We all have issues, and they affect our decision making. And PLEASE reach out to a licensed therapist or someone in the mental health field IMMEDIATELY if you are having suicidal thoughts. Call 911 if you can't find a crisis line. And remember that NO ONE is worth taking your life over!

I know the pain is devastating, and you might want to give up and end your life, but don't! You might not believe Satan exists, but he's real, and that's just what he wants you to do. He will tear you down, but God can pick you back up. God is always there for you, and He wants to help you and heal you. He loves you and wants you to be happy, so call out to Him. That crisis line is always open!

Okay, once you're past that crisis phase, and you're able to crawl out of bed, do something just for you. As I said in my advice for the betrayed woman, get a little exercise, even if it's just walking around the yard. Get cleaned up and put on your face. Get out of the house and do something you like to do—anything. Hug your children and your dog and tell them you love them. Don't hug your cat, unless you want to be bitten and scratched, but I'm sure you know that. Just give them the correct food in the correct dish at the correct time. Then maybe, if you're lucky, they'll let you touch them.

Get together with some friends. Have a drink or two IF you have a designated driver. If not, call a cab. If it's warm, go for a walk in a park or by a river. Watch the squirrels play. If it's cold, go for a drive. Jam out on your *old* favorite songs, the ones that won't remind you of him! Dance. Yes, dance! It's good exercise, and it'll release endorphins. You need them.

Pray. That also releases endorphins... more than exercise.

Loving a married man is an agonizing experience. However, it does NOT have to define you or your life. It's something you've experienced—it's NOT who you are. Don't hold onto shame that others might try to assign to you. You made a bad choice (or maybe lots of them), but you are NOT a bad person.

According to statistics, at least half the couples who get married experience infidelity, which means that there are a whole lot of broken-hearted 'other women' out there who know how you feel.

Chapter 6

Women Who Love Cheaters

How many times have you finally gained the strength to get away from an abusive, addicted cheater, only to rush into a relationship with another man who is just as bad for you, if not worse? You aren't alone. I've done it, and so have thousands of others.

This type of woman is discussed in great detail in Robin Norwood's book, *Women Who Love Too Much—When You Keep Wishing and Hoping He'll Change*. Robin describes the way these women subconsciously recreate the dynamics that were present in their childhoods, in a desperate attempt to fix what was wrong and conquer the pain. If she can change her current relationship, making the unavailable, cruel, distant, alcoholic, commitment-phobic liar love her, she feels as if she can stop the pain from her childhood that she constantly carries with her. I could've written that book myself, because I've seen these dynamics in my own relationships play out year after year.

Robin calls women who love too much *co-alcoholics*. I don't like the term *co-alcoholic*, because it is alcohol specific. It seems to imply that the addiction of the woman is only to an alcoholic. Sometimes it is. Other times, it isn't. The man to whom that kind of woman is obsessively drawn might be a drug addict, a gambling addict, a workaholic, or just a cruel, controlling unavailable man. And by unavailable, I don't necessarily mean that he's married to someone else. He might be married to the addicted woman, but still unable to commit to her—a cheater. Or he might be a man who is in prison or who lives in another state, or even another country.

I prefer to call these women *co-dependent*, which conveys a dependency, but not upon a specific type of addict. The dependency is upon the man who represents an opportunity to fix the past and take away the woman's pain. Co-dependent people seek partners who are needy in some way. He might be sick, unemployed, and addicted, or he might be a hateful, obsessive overachiever.

Regardless of the specific need of the man, the co-dependent woman sees him as someone she can help, which she believes will give her the upper hand in the relationship. She believes that in such a situation, the man will become dependent upon her, and she won't have to worry about the man leaving her. No matter how many times she sets up this type of scenario and sees it fail, she's still compelled to try it. It's all she knows.

Women Who Love Too Much is a book I've recommended to many women over the years. I first bought and read it back in 1986. It has helped me identify and leave several relationships that were causing me pain. I recognized myself in many parts of the book, and I learned to pick up on the warning signals with these men and get out before they became violent. However, because I didn't ever completely work the recovery steps given in the book, I wasn't able to avoid once again getting involved with the type of man that was sure to hurt me.

Because I hadn't been physically abused by a man since 1995, I mistakenly believed that I was healed. Actually, I think it was more about denial than being mistaken. I didn't want to put in the work it would take to dig through all the pain from my childhood and early adulthood in order to heal. I told myself that because I was able to pick up on clues that men were violent and abusive, avoiding being physically abused, I didn't need any more help with being co-dependent. I kept struggling with relationships, almost exclusively with commitment-phobic alcoholics, but still, I refused to connect the dots.

Then I talked to a woman whose life could've been a case history in *Women Who Love Too Much*. As we discussed her current relationship, I recalled quotes from the book and told her as much as I could remember, and I begged her to get the book for herself.

She talked about leaving her boyfriend and going out with a nice, decent man with whom she wished she could feel an attraction, but didn't. She said, "I just kept thinking, 'Maybe if he would call me a bitch or something....'" She was describing the way co-dependent women feel bored and uncomfortable when they try to be with a man who could care for them and treat them with respect. It struck me so hard that I bought another copy of the book.

After reading it again, I realized how desperately I still needed to work the steps. I still struggle with many, if not most, of the same issues I did all those years ago. I still carry pain from my dysfunctional childhood, along with pain from so many rejections, lies, betrayals, and attacks (physical, verbal, and emotional) from men I've loved. I've made a lot of progress, but I still have a long road ahead of me.

If you find yourself in these situations and realize that I'm talking about you, don't feel ashamed. You learned to behave the way you do, and you learned to deal with the kind of pain you've experienced. It molded you, but you aren't carved in stone. You're like clay, which can be remolded. You can work to change these old patterns of behavior and to learn new ones—healthy ones. You can learn to respect yourself and love yourself enough to be drawn to others who will also love and respect you.

Call your local bookstore and see if they have a copy. If not, they can order it for you. Or you can get the ebook or paperback at Amazon.com. But get it and read it. Work the steps, and learn how to put men out of your life who don't deserve to be in it.

Embarrassment & Humiliation

Probably the most embarrassing, ultimate humiliation with regard to infidelity would be to answer the door in your sweats, hair in a ponytail and no makeup, only to find your partner's lover standing there, looking like she stepped off the cover of *Vogue*. She tells you she's sleeping with your man, and you want to die.

I haven't had that happen, thank God, but I've had the fear of that happening for more than half my life! After the things I've seen and had happen to me, it seems like that wouldn't be out of the realm of possibility. I would definitely want to know if my man were cheating, but I'd prefer a phone call. I no longer do my makeup first thing every morning, so showing up at my door without warning is frowned upon, even from friends or family.

I always knew my first husband was with other women. I found clues, and he was constantly lying, not where he was supposed to be, coming home late, going out "with the guys," coming home drunk at 2:00 or 3:00 in the morning, and that kind of thing. That was bad. But after we divorced, people were coming out of the woodwork, telling me about his cheating. It seemed that everyone in town knew it. Even my own brother knew it! I was so embarrassed.

At the mall one day, a beautiful young woman walked up to me and said, "You're *** *******'s wife, aren't you?" I said, "Yes." She said, "I thought so." Then she and her friend looked at each other and walked off. At the time, I was annoyed, because people always seemed to be in my business, interested in what I was doing. But now that I look back on it, I'm pretty sure she was one of the women he was fooling around with. She had this smug little look on her face, like she knew something I didn't know. Yep, I knew, and so did everyone else.

One reason that people don't talk with others about infidelity within their relationships is because of the embarrassment and humiliation they feel. You feel like a fool. You don't want to admit that something so horrible could happen within your relationship, especially if you're always posting photos on social media of you and your partner, talking about how much you love him and how you're the perfect couple, and he's the perfect man. Nothing can burst that 'perfect couple' bubble faster than finding that your man has cheated.

But face it. No one really believes that stuff anyway. First, we all know that no one, nor any couple, is perfect. We all have flaws, and every relationship has its problems. And remember that most of us know exactly how you feel, because we've been through it, too. If we haven't had someone cheat on us, either we've been the other woman or the cheater. Or maybe all three. There is probably no one who hasn't been affected by infidelity in some way.

Honestly, I've found that unless you're a constant whiner, always complaining about something, people respond in a positive way when they know you're hurting. They are sympathetic, and if they have something to offer you in the way of advice, they are quick to share it. They're sorry to hear that you're hurting, but at the same time, knowing about your misfortune might help them to not feel so bad about their own issues and pain. Misery loves company. It's good to know that you're not alone... and you're not. We know how you feel, and we care.

Okay, you're right. Not everyone cares. There might be a few jealous, hateful, cruel trolls out there who might be happy to know you're hurting. But why waste precious seconds of your life thinking about what they might do, say, think, or feel? Does it make any sense to keep your problems and your pain all bottled up, just because you're worried that someone might enjoy hearing about it? That's your pride talking. Don't listen.

I'm not saying that you should showcase your dirty laundry all over your social media pages. People don't want to read all the sordid details, and they certainly don't want to read page-long rants directed at your partner or his other woman! I hate that, and when I see it, I usually 'unfollow' the person, hiding their posts. Keep that private. But if you let people know in a dignified way that you're hurting because of your partner's infidelity, people will rush to your rescue, because they know what you're going through, and they sympathize with you.

On the other hand, there is something to take into account before broadcasting the news that your man cheated. If you think you might stay with him, you have to know that if you tell family and friends that he hurt you, they won't be as quick to welcome him back with open arms as you are. They don't feel about him the way you do, so it'll be hard for them to be around him after they find out what he's done.

What's more, even though you decided to forgive him and try to make it work, it's not fair for you to expect your loved ones to be so accepting of him. Your emotions are playing a big part in your decision making, which is why counseling is so important. But their feelings about him aren't tainted by chemistry, romance, and memories of great sex and love. Even if they hope you can work it out, because they think that's best for your children, they fear that you might be making a mistake if you stay together, as they don't want to see you hurt again.

"Once a cheater, always a cheater." You'll hear that from your loved ones. It makes you want to crawl under something and die... or scream. Though that's not always true, it is in some cases, if not most. If he cheats, and you hold onto him, where's the deterrent to keep him from doing it again?

Please understand that I would never suggest that you end a good relationship because of feelings of embarrassment. But how good is the relationship if he saw fit to betray you? How good is it if he was okay with gratifying his own selfish sexual desires, knowing that if you found out, you would be crushed?

Maybe those feelings of humiliation and embarrassment are telling you something. They're there for a reason. Well, part of it is pride, which is not good, but that's not what I'm talking about. We are born with certain feelings that are inherent in knowing what is good for us and what is bad for us. Aside from the pain of being betrayed, you also feel humiliated and embarrassed, because he disrespected you in one of the worst ways possible.

These feelings are all completely normal. I can't imagine anyone in your shoes who wouldn't feel the same way. But remind yourself that you have nothing to be ashamed of. And being humbled doesn't feel good, but it doesn't have to be bad. It reminds us of the fact that nothing is guaranteed, and we are not above failing. That doesn't sound like a good thing, but it can be. It reminds us to count our blessings and remember where they came from. It reminds us to not take things for granted, and that's a good thing.

Unforgiveness Is a Cancer

Your heart is broken. You don't want to forgive them. You think they don't deserve to be forgiven. But here's the thing: *It's not for them! It's for you!* Forgiving those who hurt and wronged us is the most important step when it comes to healing our own minds, spirits, and hearts.

Sometimes we hold onto all those awful feelings and refuse to forgive, because we think of it as punishment for those who hurt us. But does it work? I mean, have you ever had a guy toward whom you were holding bad feelings come up to you and say, "Please! You've gotta stop feeling this way! It's killing my new girlfriend and me that you're resentful, bitter, and full of rage!" Doubtful.

Unforgiveness eats away at your soul like a cancer. It grows and grows, until you're so filled with hate and rage that no one can see past it. I held onto it until I was exhausted. It turned me into someone I don't even recognize now. I thought that if I held onto all that ugliness, somehow it would protect me from being hurt, but guess what! It did the exact opposite. It guaranteed that I hurt every day because of past betrayals. Not only that, but I also got hurt over and over again from new guys, which was proof that unforgiveness doesn't protect you from anything!

When someone cheats on you, either you move on, or you (meaning both of you) try to hold on and work it out. If you try to stay together, and you (meaning you alone) can't forgive, you have ZERO chance of working it out. If you move on, and you can't forgive, you have ZERO chance of making it work with someone else! Why? Because that bitterness and rage will cause you to punish the next guy who comes along. You might not even realize you're doing it, but you will. I wish I had a dime for every time a guy said to me, "Stop beating me up for what *he* did to you! I didn't do it! He did!"

I'm not saying you should throw caution to the wind and give yourself 100% to the next guy who comes along. To the contrary—you should be cautious. And you should look for signs that the next guy is worthy of your trust *before* you give it. But if you want to give a relationship a chance, you can't blame the new guy for what the last guy did. You know he didn't do those things to you, but it's like you have to punish him just in case he's going to. But is that fair? And does it work? I should know. I was the queen of unforgiveness! It doesn't work!

It wasn't until I was in therapy years ago that I learned about it—forgiving others, as well as forgiving myself. I didn't really understand what it was. I thought it meant saying that what the offending person did was okay, and it wasn't, and I wasn't gonna say it was! But that's not what forgiveness is. It means that you're making a decision to give up those awful feelings you're holding onto that are eating you up inside. You know, those feelings that make you sometimes feel like you're going to puke, but don't do a thing to him? Yeah, those.

Forgiving also means that you give up any 'right' or opportunity to get revenge upon him (and her) for what he did. That's a tough one. I know you want to hurt him back. And I know you think it would make you feel good, and it might—at that moment. But later on, when you had time to cool down, if you really love him, you'd feel bad about hurting him. Okay, you think he deserves it, but does he? Are we so perfect that we should have the right to judge others so harshly?

The next two paragraphs are about my experience with forgiveness with regard to my faith. If you don't have that faith, you can still benefit from the following message.

When I found Jesus, I began to understand how important forgiveness is. The Bible tells us that if we don't forgive others, *God won't forgive us* for our sins. That's powerful! When I first read that, my heart almost pounded out of my chest! I knew I was in trouble, so I started praying all the time for God to put forgiveness in my heart for the people who had hurt me. I told Him that I was making a conscious decision to forgive these people, and I stopped obsessing over what they had done to me and how I could get back at them. I put those things out of my mind. And it began to happen. Gradually, those awful feelings began to fade.

Another thing that made a huge difference in my life was a scripture that scared me. You've heard it. "Judge not, lest ye be judged." In today's language, it means, "You'll be judged by the same measure to which you judge others." So if you think he doesn't deserve to be forgiven, as far as God is concerned, neither do you. Those are profound words, and they made a drastic change in the way I feel toward others. We all have many things that we need to be forgiven for, so we really need to forgive others, as well as ourselves.

It's hard not to judge others, but you have to train your mind to not go there. And it doesn't mean you're okay with what they did. It means that you're not willing to flip the switch on the electric chair.

Forgiving him also does not mean that you have to stay with him or go back to him! You do not have to grant someone who hurt you the opportunity to do it again, just because you choose to forgive him. As I said before, it's not about him. It's about healing your own heart and being able to go on with your life with joy, rather than resentment and hate.

Have you ever thought of the amount of time, effort, and energy you waste on hating and raging about things people have done to hurt you? Have you thought about how much good you could do for yourself and others if you used all that time, effort, and energy toward something positive?

If you'll trust me on this and let go of the hate and unforgiveness, you'll see what I mean. Your heart will feel so much lighter, and that grimace will leave your face. You'll smile, your depression will lessen, or maybe even disappear completely, and you'll even look younger! (Frowns make you look older.)

If you want to feel better for you, forgiving is something you need to work on. First, forgive yourself for your own sins, mistakes, and bad decisions. Stop beating yourself up! And then start working on forgiving others. It's usually a process that takes some time, and if you're used to holding onto those old painful feelings, you're probably going to need help. God will put forgiveness in your heart if you'll pray sincerely for it and open your heart to receive it. You can do it. Trust me! If I can do it, anyone can do it!

Another thing to consider is that if you go out with that angry grimace on your face, you'll be the biggest jerk-magnet in town. I know—I've been that girl. But after you've learned to forgive others and yourself, you'll be in a much better place mentally, spiritually, and emotionally. Then you'll be more likely to attract the kind of person who won't hurt you. Healthy people are attracted to healthy people. Do whatever you have to do to get healthy in all those ways. I suggest God and therapy, but that's your decision. Do whatever it takes, because you deserve to be happy, and forgiveness is the key to happiness.

Consumed By Hate

When I say "hate," I'm not talking about merely disliking someone. I'm talking about having intense feelings toward someone to the point that you want to hurt that person. Rage usually goes along with hatred. It can drain you of energy, it can make you sick, and it seriously damages you spiritually. In fact, it can destroy you.

It's easy to see how you could feel that way about someone who constantly does things that cause you pain, but who does that help? Or who does it hurt? It doesn't hurt the person you hate. Most of the time, that person will hate you, too, so it doesn't matter to him (or her) that you feel that way. It probably only makes that person feel justified in whatever he's doing that hurts you. No, the hate mainly hurts the person who feels it.

It goes hand in hand with unforgiveness in most situations. It's a feeling that can completely consume you, and it robs you of your peace and happiness.

You're probably thinking, *No, HE (or she) robs me of my peace and happiness!* But, as I learned in therapy, people cannot take your peace if you don't let them. You do that yourself when you choose to hold onto hate and unforgiveness.

Your feelings are your own choices. When I first heard that, I thought it was crazy. I thought I couldn't control the way I felt—that I was subject to my feelings. But the truth is that our feelings are controlled by our thoughts.

Here's an extreme example, so you can see what I mean: Let's say that there was a guy you knew who was convicted of murder. You don't know whether this person is guilty or not, but you never would've imagined he could kill someone. You would probably distance yourself from him, and you would definitely not think of this person as a potential mate for many reasons. But there are some people whose hearts would go out to the guy. They would see him as a victim and be drawn to him. Yeah, they probably have their own issues, but the point is this: The difference in the way a person feels about something or someone is all in their perception. It's in the way they think about it.

Many, if not most, betrayed women tend to be consumed with hate and rage toward the other woman. Somehow, they manage to forgive, or at least get past, what their partners did by cheating, but they hold onto their hate for the women they choose to see as the reason their world fell apart. Once again, remember who it was that cheated on you! Then, look at the intent. That works in any situation—not just infidelity.

When you believe that someone has wronged you, look at the intent. If she (or he) didn't hurt you on purpose, it doesn't mean that it doesn't hurt or that it's okay. But it means that your pain was not something she wanted or intentionally created. Whatever she did wasn't done with malice toward you. She didn't mean to hurt you. Sometimes the person who hurts you feels terrible about the fact that what she did caused others to hurt. You might not think it matters, but it does.

Let's look at another example: Say you're playing softball, and a friend throws the ball and accidentally hits you. She runs over and tells you she's sorry, and she checks to make sure you're okay. Now, let's say you're playing softball with another team, and on that team is a girl who has hated you since elementary school. She throws the ball as hard as she can, and it hits you. You see the look on her face, and you know it was intentional.

In both cases, you were hit by a ball. But one person *wanted* to hurt you, and the other didn't. It makes no sense to hate the person who accidentally hit you. Does it? As for the one who hit you intentionally, you could hate her, but what would that accomplish?

The best thing you could do is to tell her there are no hard feelings and smile. Not a wicked smile, but a sincere one. It might change her feelings toward you, and all the hate could go away. Wouldn't that be cool? That probably wouldn't happen. But it would at least make her think about you as a person, and she might actually rethink her feelings toward you. If nothing else, she would see that you are above the hate and are not willing to stoop to her level.

I once met a woman in a community college I attended, and we became friends. One day, she was telling me that I was nothing like she thought I would be. She said, "Gah, Kitten! If people would just get to know you, they wouldn't think you were a bitch!" I laughed. "Thanks... I think." She might as well have said, "Everybody thinks you're a bitch and hates you." I didn't even know those people! You might be thinking I must've been snobby or rude, but I wasn't. I always smiled at people, but I was rather shy. I usually didn't talk to people I didn't know, which was everyone there, except that one woman. I was open to them, but Brenda was the only one who approached me.

Another similar instance was on my first day at a new high school—10th grade. A guy walked up to me and said, "Cathy ******* hates you." I said, "Who is she?" He told me she was just a girl and that she was probably jealous. Since I had never met her, I had obviously never done anything to anger her, but she despised me all throughout the next three years! She might even hate me now, for all I know.

I'm sensitive about this subject because of my experiences with so many women who have hated me for no apparent reason. There are others who did have reasons to have bad feelings toward me. But some of these women still feel that way many years after the incidents took place. I understand it, and I don't hate them, but I wish that for their own good, they would let it go. Holding onto the hate doesn't help them in any way—it only hurts them. I'm asking you now, please forgive me.

I wish I could change the things I've done that hurt others. I wouldn't want to change everything I did, but I definitely wish that what I did hadn't caused pain for anyone. And I would like for them to know that I'm not the monster they think I am. I've said and done many things that I wish I could take back and change, and for those things, I'm sorry. I hope that these people can forgive me, get past their hatred, and heal their own hearts.

People are so quick to point out the sins of others, but they don't see their own sins. There's a scripture that talks about that. Matthew 7:5 says (paraphrased), "Hypocrite, first take the plank out of your own eye, and then you can see to remove the splinter from your brother's eye." In other words, fix what's wrong with yourself before you try to fix what's wrong with someone else.

When you stop to think that we are not sinless, you should remember that includes all of us. John 8:7 says (paraphrased), "Let the sinless one cast the first stone." In case you aren't familiar with the scripture, Jesus is telling these guys who want to stone a woman to death for adultery that the one who is without sin should be the first to throw a rock at her. No one is without sin, so no one could throw that rock.

There was one thing that made me work really hard to not hate. 1 John 3:15 says (paraphrased) that if you hate your 'brother' (which means anyone), you are a murderer and that no murderer has eternal life abiding in him. When I read that, I was shocked! So if you hate someone, you are guilty of murder. That scared me, and it made me think long and hard about the way I felt about people who had hurt me, whether they meant to or not.

When I started to make changes in my thoughts, I began to see these people as human beings, not as monsters. My feelings began to change, and the hatred gradually faded. I couldn't believe the difference in the way it made me feel. It was amazing!

I didn't mean to preach a sermon in this section. I just know that those scriptures had a major impact on the way I felt about people, especially those who had hurt me. And I'm hoping that if you think about those things, they will help you change your ways of thinking, too. Remember that our feelings are controlled by our thoughts. If we think hateful thoughts, we feel hatred. If we think loving and kind thoughts, we feel love.

I can't say that I don't have any bad feelings at all, though I try not to. But I can say that I don't hate anyone. There is no one that I would harm physically, given the chance. There is no one that I would harm mentally or emotionally, given the chance. At least, I believe that's true.

If you are full of hatred, please take under advisement the things you've just read. Think about what the Bible says about it. Look it up if you don't believe me. Think about the fact that your thoughts control your feelings. Try to think of these people and their actions. Maybe they didn't mean to hurt you. But even if they did, you still don't have to hate them. I'm telling you this for your own wellbeing. Especially if you have children, it's not good for them to see your bitterness and hatred. That only teaches them to feel it, too, and I know you don't want that for them.

If you can't control your rage, look into anger management counseling or classes. I knew a girl years ago who had gone to see her boyfriend late at night and found a girl with him. She attacked him and the girl. They called the police and pressed charges, and my friend was arrested. The court ordered her to go to the classes, and *she said it was the best thing that had ever happened to her.* She learned how to cope with her anger, and to my knowledge, she never attacked anyone else.

Just remember that we're human. We all make mistakes. We do things we regret. We do things we're ashamed of. We all do it. None of us is perfect, and we deserve to be forgiven. Try to think of it that way, and work on putting away the hatred. You won't believe how much better you'll feel when you stop carrying around all those horrible feelings. That's a lot of really heavy baggage you can leave right where it is and never have to pick it up again.

Chapter 7

The Children

When you get those butterflies in your stomach, because he just walked into the room, the last thing you're thinking about is children. When he brushes against you in the breakroom, you aren't thinking about what could happen if you responded. When he gets around to kissing you, all you can think about is how much you want him. Children—yours or his—are not on your radar.

It's not that you don't care about how your behavior will affect them. Of course, you care. And it's not that he doesn't care. He cares, too. It's just that when those endorphins start flooding your brain, and your body is tingling all over, though there's a battle going on in your mind, certain body parts become 'the boss of you.' They make your decisions for you.

Oh, man, he smells good! No, I can't. Breathe, breathe! His eyes are soooo blue. He's killing me. But what about Billy? What if he finds out? Oh, that feels so good! He won't find out. Okay, just this one time. But if Billy finds out, what would that do to the...? Oh, that's good. Yeah, right there...

If you go through with it, eventually your head clears from the fog of hormones that rendered you temporarily insane. That's when reality kicks in, and you see what you've done. *What the hell was I thinking?*

He's probably going through the same scenarios in his mind. *She finds out, I'm screwed. She'll take everything. She'll take the kids. I'm so stupid! What the hell was I thinking? Okay, I know what I was thinking, but now what do I do? How do I get out of this?*

You both come to your senses and resolve to never let it happen again, promising yourselves to think about your families the next time you see each other. But then the fear of losing everything starts to fade. And the memory of that encounter seeps into your conscious thoughts again… and again… and again…. He has to call. He does, and when you see it's him, your heart skips a beat, and then it pounds. It's on.

Never, at any moment, did either of you think that hurting the children, either his or yours, was all right. It sounds like a copout, but the reality is that when your hormones take over, the way they do when you begin a romantic and/or sexual relationship with someone, it's difficult to think of anything other than that person. It's not a lack of caring about others on either part. It's a matter of being overwhelmed with emotions and physical sensations to the point that you temporarily lose sight of the consequences of your actions.

Still, when you get caught, people suffer. He's thinking that his wife won't find out, but if she did, she'd be upset, but she'd be okay. You're thinking the same about your husband. But you're both concerned for the wellbeing of your children. Neither of you wants to hurt anyone, but you are certain that if discovered, there will be a tsunami of tears all around.

I know what it's like to be caught up in emotions and do things that hurt people. It was NEVER my intention to cause anyone to suffer, but because I fell in love with the wrong men, people were hurt. And some of those people were children. I hate that! I'm so sorry for that!

It also bothers me to think that women were hurt. I know what it feels like to be cheated on. I've been betrayed. I'm familiar with the rage and the agony. I know how it feels to want to hold onto him and strangle him to death at the same time.

But more than that, I feel for the children. I'm sure that would ring hollow to those who were hurt, but all I can do is write about how I feel. I actually know a little bit about how that feels, too. When I was a child, I remember hearing my parents fight over my father's infidelity. I remember being confused about it, not understanding what they were talking about. As I got older, I picked up on the fact that Dad had been with other women. Plural.

My dad and I were never close, so I didn't really fear his leaving. But I hated to see my mom so upset, and I hated him for hurting her. He never left Mom, but from what I understand, as long as he had opportunities, he took advantage of them.

When my mom found out about the married man and me, she told me about the one time she had cheated on my dad. After many years of living with emotional abuse, neglect by my dad, and being completely faithful to him, she met someone who seemed to care about her. And she allowed herself to get involved with him.

It didn't bother me, because by then, my parents' relationship had deteriorated to the point that if they weren't arguing, there was a deafening silence that pervaded the house. And between my father and me, it was an almost constant battle. It was bad. There were many dynamics that contributed to the dysfunction in our family, but infidelity was always a part of it.

As a child, probably around 13 years old, I remember lying on my bed, thinking about the fact that someday, I would be in love with a married man. It wasn't something I wanted—it was something I just knew. I dreaded it. I knew it would be awful, but I had no doubt that it was going to happen. I'm sure it had something to do with hearing my parents fight over Dad's cheating, but that wasn't a conscious connection at the time. It was more like a feeling.

Because of the way my dad's infidelity affected me, I hate to think of the effect a couple of my relationships had on children. I'm terribly sorry about that, and I wish I could change it. I won't, however, take responsibility for the actions of the men who did the cheating. I never seduced a man. I didn't have to. They were the pursuers, the liars, and the cheaters. I was the foolish one who believed their lies.

Men who blame their lovers for their own bad choices are cowards. In doing that, they teach their children to be cowards and pass the buck as they did.

I hope this doesn't sound as if I'm saying it's okay to be unfaithful to your partner and to hurt your children. I do understand how it happens, and that when it does happen, it isn't meant to hurt anyone, most especially not the children. But I also know what it's like to be a child in the midst of a family in turmoil because of infidelity (among other things). It does affect children. There's no denying that. But it doesn't have to destroy them. I survived, though scarred, and millions of others do, too.

If you are a child who was hurt by the infidelity of one or both of your parents, please let go of the hate and resentment. I know it hurts, but by holding onto those feelings, you're hurting yourself. It'll eat you up inside and destroy the joy and happiness God wants for you if you allow it to. It will also affect your own relationships in a bad way. It comes down to forgiveness. I know you don't want to forgive, especially the other woman or other man, but in order to make yourself feel better, that's what you have to do. PLEASE get help if you're not able to do it on your own. Do it for yourself, your own children, and your future.

Parents, if you've been unfaithful, and you see that it's affecting your children, don't wait. Take them to a therapist before those negative emotions do more damage. And make sure the children know that they are in no way responsible for your cheating. They tend to think it's their fault, so it's up to you to correct that error in their thoughts.

Even if you don't see evidence that your children are being affected, know that they are. A friend of mine told me that she had cheated on her husband years ago. Now, she's afraid that her grown daughter is doing the same thing. She's torn, because she doesn't want to see her daughter make that mistake.

People have always cheated. They always will. Partners will be hurt. Children will be hurt. The ones with whom people cheat will be hurt. Families and friends will be hurt. It's not okay, but it's reality.

If you're already in love with someone else, and you want to build a life with that person, you might believe it's worth the pain it would

116

cause to your loved ones, to the one you want to be with, and to yourself. But don't underestimate that pain. And don't think it'll only be for a few weeks or months, and then you'll have The Brady Bunch. Sometimes the hate, rage, and unforgiveness last for many years. In some cases, it's never resolved. Remember that. Only you can make that decision.

And if you're planning to leave, please be careful about how you tell the children. Don't let them hear you screaming at each other about it as you're walking out the door. Put your bitterness and anger aside for the sake of the kids. Sit them down and explain it in a mature, caring way. Also, be careful about the timing of the revelation. Make sure it's not on or near their birthdays or the holidays. I know a couple who told their children they were divorcing on Christmas Day! Merry freakin' Christmas!

On the other hand, if you're only caught up in the sexual intensity, with no ideas of ever having a relationship with that person, please stop to think about the possible ramifications of your actions. Don't assume you won't get caught. Instead, assume that you *will* be caught, because there's a good chance of that. Think about the agony it will bring and the damage you will cause to your family, just for a few hours (or minutes) of sexual gratification. Is the sex worth all the carnage? Think about the children. Don't do it.

The Families, Friends, & Pets

As you well know, it's not just the cheater, the betrayed, the other woman, and the children who are affected when someone is unfaithful—especially if he leaves. The families and friends on both sides are also hurt and angry, and they are put in the position of having to take sides.

MOST families stand by their own, regardless of which side of the triangle the family member is on. If the friends were around before the couple got together, most of the time, the one who knew the friends first 'gets custody.' However, friends are in a situation where there is no real right thing to do if they are friends with the cheater and the betrayed. If the friends continue to associate with the cheater, the betrayed feels further betrayed. If the friends remain in touch with the betrayed, the cheater feels uncomfortable with those friends.

Especially around holidays, when families and friends get together to celebrate, infidelity creates a serious problem. Even if the couple is still together, family members and friends can't ignore their own feelings about the issue. I think that in the interest of peace, mainly for the children in the family, people usually try to be civil, when they really want to go off on the cheater. But in some homes, that doesn't happen. Some people are more emotional and are unable to hold in their anger, especially when they either see or perceive the pain of the children. It can easily spiral out of control and become a Jerry Springer moment. Someone calls 911, and they all hope they won't end up on the evening news.

The parents of the couple are in a particularly difficult predicament. They usually love them both and desperately want them to work things out, but at the same time, they have anger and resentment toward the cheater. And the longer the couple has been together, the harder it is on everyone involved.

And don't forget about the little furry babies. People don't think about their emotions so much, but they are real. They love their families, and when there is tension, they suffer, too. Or even more, if someone is missing, they experience heartache and grief, just like we do—only they don't understand what's going on.

The last time I took Peej (my little dachshund who passed away on September 26, 2014) to Muscle Shoals to visit my mom and my daughter, she was grieving over being away from my husband. She looked so pitiful and had tears in her eyes that first night we were there. One little tear actually pooled and rolled over her bottom right lid. It breaks my heart to know that she was so sad, missing him, before she passed. (Oh, how I grieve for her!)

I've seen infidelity cause catastrophic damage. I know a family who has experienced a bit of recovery lately, but only after about six years of rage, verbal attacks, threats, and emotional distance. Some of that damage will never be repaired. It's an extreme case, and it didn't have to be that way, but it does happen.

As with the children, don't think that everyone will be upset for a little while, but then it'll all work out. Sometimes it doesn't work out. Sometimes family members go years, or even the rest of their lives, without speaking. I can't tell you what to do, but please consider ALL the collateral damage before you allow yourself to do something you'll probably regret.

Chapter 8

How to Get Over a Cheater

Getting over any man you love obviously won't be easy. And unfortunately, I don't have a magic recovery pill. I wish I did. But learning how to deal with anything is all in your perception of it.

If you think of him as your soulmate, someone you can't live without, you won't ever be able to let him go, much less get over him. Think reality. Below are some suggestions that are sure to help *once you've made the decision to get rid of him*. I know this, because they have helped me.

Face the facts.

Girls, whether you are his partner or his other woman, the man is cheating on you! That man does not deserve to have you and another woman, no matter how awesome you think he is. I don't care if he's a good father, a millionaire, or the best-looking guy you've ever seen… or all of those things and more! You're not doing yourself or your children any favors by staying with a man who doesn't love and respect you. And if he truly loved and respected you, he wouldn't be involved with another woman. Facing that reality will help with the following steps.

Stop communicating with him.

You have a lot of thinking to do and a lot of decisions to make with regard to where you're going to live, how to handle the finances, child visitation, etc. You can't see what's best for you while he's trying to get you to focus on what's best for him, which is *always* his first priority. In his mind, it's all about him. He's a narcissist. Don't let it be all about him in your mind, too. Make it about you. Somebody has to, and it won't be him!

I'm NOT suggesting that you keep his children from him. NEVER use them to punish him, because though you might think he deserves it, the children do not. Have a friend or family member talk to him with regard to visitation, what they need, and things like that.

Put your feelings for him aside.

You can't possibly dismantle your relationship and get over him if you stay in that foggy state we think of as love. I call it *crazy mode*. It's not really love. If you're involved with a man who is emotionally and/or sexually involved with another woman, there are very unhealthy dynamics in play, and though there might be some love in the mix, odds are more in favor of obsession.

Regardless of whether or not there is true love on your part, remember (again) that if he truly loved you, he wouldn't be with her. Feelings are too difficult to define or measure, and they can and usually do change. They are unreliable, so do your best to not look at them *once you've made the decision to end the relationship.*

Look at what the relationship is doing to you.

Ask yourself how your life has changed since he has been a part of it. How have your mood, personality, energy level, and outlook on life changed because of him?

It's practically impossible to be involved with a cheater and not experience some level of depression. Some women even think about suicide. Some have actually taken their own lives because of the intense pain they felt while loving a cheating man. Hey, he's not worth it! You have a life to live, and he's apparently not supposed to be a part of it if this is how he makes you feel. Don't fool yourself.

Make a 'cons' list.

In case you didn't start that list when you read it earlier in the book, do it now! It's crucial! Notice that I didn't say "a pros and cons list." That's because you need to put any positive things about him out of your mind. No one is 100% bad or 100% good. Even the most evil people might have some redeeming qualities, but that doesn't mean they're good for you.

List every negative personality trait, physical trait, every time he's ever done or said anything that hurt you, and anything at all that you don't like about him or your situation. I know it hurts, but this is a really important step. Don't just think about it—write it down. It needs to be tangible, something you can hold in your hand and look at. Keep that list with you constantly and add anything that isn't already on it. It's easier to realize it and accept it if you write it down.

Be totally honest with yourself about him. This is no time to be nice or politically correct. If you think his head is too big for his body, put that on your list. If he said you need to watch your weight, add that to the list and include how that made you feel.

Study what you've written about him.

Read that list over and over again. Every time you feel weak, pull it out and read it again. Think about each thing you wrote. Allow yourself to feel the pain associated with each of the things you put on the list. That pain is telling you that this relationship is BAD for you. Loving someone shouldn't hurt like that.

Think about the way you feel every time he walks out your door, when you think (or know) that he's going to see her or to go home to his wife. Do you really think you deserve to be treated that way? How dare he do that to you? Who does he think he is?

Get angry!

Notice that I didn't say, "Hate him," or, "Never forgive him," or, "Stay angry for the rest of your life." Justified anger is not just okay, but it's good for a time. It moves us to change things that hurt us, which is why God gave us that emotion.

Think about the arrogance it takes to keep one woman at home to cook, clean, wash his clothes, take care of his children, and care for his home, while having another woman on the side for his romantic, sexual pleasure! He doesn't have the right to lie to and cheat on his wife, but he also doesn't have the right to lie to, cheat on, and use another woman.

No woman deserves to be treated disrespectfully. Whether you're his partner or his other woman, you deserve to have a man who loves, adores, and respects you enough to resist the temptations of other women. It's time for you to see him for the disrespectful, arrogant man that he is!

You don't love *him*! You love the man you *thought* he was! If you're his wife of many years, maybe you love the man he *used to* be, but more likely, just as the other woman, you love the man you *imagined* he was.

It's time to start loving and respecting yourself, and when you do that, you won't want to hold onto a man who doesn't treat you with the utmost love and respect. If he can't treat you the way you deserve to be treated, HE DOESN'T DESERVE TO BE WITH YOU!

Get rid of him!

Make up your mind that you are ready to stop being a doormat, and start being the strong, beautiful—inside and out—woman that you were created to be, and send him packing! (Ladies, if you are married to cheaters, you'll have to file for divorce before you can have him removed from the house. There are legal issues to deal with, so speak with an attorney BEFORE you take this step.)

If he calls you, do NOT answer! If he leaves a voice mail, DELETE IT! If you listen to it, you'll only be confused, so don't do that to yourself. Same goes for texts—don't read them. Delete them! If he leaves a note on your car, rip it up. If he shows up at your house, tell him through the CLOSED door to leave, or you will have him arrested. If he doesn't leave, call the police! If he cries, just remember all the times you've cried over him. It's about time he learns how it feels to lose someone he loves.

You're thinking, *What if there's an emergency?* Is he not smart enough to get someone else to contact you in case of an emergency? If not, there's another reason to get over him.

Consider him dead.

That sounds harsh, but what I mean is that you should put him that far out of your life. Dead men can't talk, text, or type, so as I said before, ignore them all. But in this step, you need to let yourself grieve. If you have to pull out pictures of him and stick pins in them or burn them, go for it. If you have to cry until your eyes are swollen shut, with tiny little blood spots on your lids (been there), that's okay. If you have to get rid of every material thing that reminds you of him (aside from the kids), which I highly recommend, get busy. Grieve the death of the relationship, bury it, and move on.

Don't look back.

This one's really difficult, but you can do it. For me, the key to this step was to realize that the man I thought I loved so much didn't really exist! I loved a man who, *in my mind*, was kind, generous, loving, devoted to me, 'faithful' to me, and honest…. After years of suffering, I realized that he was none of the above! He had his moments, but overall, he was a completely different person than the guy I thought he was. I had focused on those moments, rather than looking at the days, months, and years of his being a real jerk.

When you have a weak moment (or night), pull out that cons list and read everything you wrote about him. Remember every time he was with her. Remember every time he made you feel like you weren't good enough. Remember every condescending word he ever said to you. Remember every lie. Remember every broken promise and every time he said he'd be there but wasn't, because something more important came up, like his wife's parents coming over for dinner. Surely, you don't want to contact HIM!

Then remember that the sweet, caring, faithful man you love so much is nothing more than a figment of your imagination. No matter how weak you feel, you can't contact someone who doesn't exist, so don't let yourself go there. Don't allow yourself to think about it, even if it's Christmas Eve, Christmas night, New Year's Eve, Valentine's Day, or your birthday. There are lots of worse things in the world than being alone, including being with someone who hurts you.

But *when* that weak moment comes, and it will, and you go there in your mind, remind yourself of how horrible he made you feel.

Remember the betrayal, the lies, and the humiliation. Think of the hours of sobbing, because you know he's with her, and even worse, he loves her. It won't take you long to realize that you're not longing for HIM. You're longing for SOMEONE—the guy you THOUGHT he was.

Move on.

The first step toward moving on, as I've spelled out for you before, is to forgive both the cheater and the other woman (or women) he's been with. And don't forget to also forgive yourself for ignoring the signs, being in denial, and loving the man you *wanted* him to be. (If you're the other woman, that would mean forgiving the cheater, as well as yourself.) This might take a while, but if you don't do it, you're only hurting yourself.

Once you've done all the other steps, it's time to experience life without him. It's okay if you feel uncomfortable. You've seen yourself as *his* for a long time, and it'll take a while to adjust, but you can do it. You feel needy right now, but no matter what you do—do not let it show! Do not let your anger show! Do not let your pain show! Save all that for your therapist, your girlfriends, or your support group.

It's not easy to start over, so just take baby steps. You're not ready for another relationship! It's scary to be alone, and you're probably thinking of calling an old flame, but if you do, you're going to be jumping from the frying pan, right into the fire! Think about that. 'Flame' is a good description for a guy who probably burned you in the past, huh?

The same goes for a new guy. You'll be tempted to find someone new in order to distract yourself and focus on someone else to ease the pain, but it won't work. You'll find another guy like the one you're trying to get over, so how can that help? It can't. And distracting yourself from the pain to that degree could actually delay your healing. I hate to say it, but you really need to feel that pain and trudge on through it. It's part of the process of getting over someone.

You need to nurture yourself and find that strong, confident woman you used to be. Or if you were never that strong, confident woman, now is the time to work on becoming that woman.

*Read *Women Who Love Too Much* by Robin Norwood.*
I've told you about this book before, but I'm including it in this step, because I believe it's that important. In order to keep from repeating the same relationship mistakes you've made before, you need to understand why you do the things you do and how to change those things. *WWLTM* is an excellent resource for that purpose.

Get some therapy.
Okay, I know I sound like a broken record (some of you might be 'mature' enough to know what that means) with the therapy thing. Sorry. But because I know that some of you might not read all parts of the book, I don't want to take the chance that anyone would miss this step. Maybe I should've listed this as the first step. It can help you, regardless of where you are in the process of dealing with all your emotional pain.

When you find that your man has been unfaithful, it shatters your self-esteem, it makes you doubt yourself and your own judgment, and it destroys your sense of security. You definitely need some help in getting back on your feet. Having an unbiased opinion from a therapist can be extremely helpful in getting yourself back on track. Give it a try, and you'll see what I mean.

Affirmations

It might seem silly if you've never done it before, but it's important that you say these affirmations aloud, regardless of whether or not you believe them. If you say them enough, you will begin to believe them, and they will help you to increase your self-esteem and to accept the fact that you are NOT a bad person, no matter what your position in the love triangle.

Affirmations for the Betrayed

* I am a worthwhile person.

* I am not damaged goods.

* I am a loving, caring person.

* I do not deserve to have a partner be unfaithful to me.

* I do not deserve to be used or taken for granted.

* I have done things I regret, but so has everyone else.

* I have sinned, but so has everyone else.

* I have asked for forgiveness of my sins, so I am forgiven.

* I do not hate anyone, including my partner, who cheated on me, or the person with whom he cheated. Hating them would only hurt me.

* If my partner gave valid reasons for the infidelity, and there is something I can do to make those things better, I will do so if I choose to continue in the relationship.

* Even if my partner gave valid reasons for his infidelity, he is still responsible for his own actions. It is not my fault, nor the fault of the other woman, that he cheated.

* I choose to forgive my partner and the person with whom he cheated—not for them, but for my own sake.

* I will determine what to do about the infidelity based upon what is best for me—not based upon what my partner wants.

* I affirm that staying in a relationship in which my partner cheats is not good for me or for my children.

* I understand that adultery is the only reason the Bible gives as a cause for divorce, which means that it IS important, regardless of what anyone else says.

* I deserve to be respected and appreciated.

* I deserve to be loved and wanted.

* I deserve to have my partner care enough about my feelings to not cheat on me.

* I will no longer allow myself to be treated disrespectfully, because I deserve better.

* I will stand up for my right to be loved and appreciated.

* I will not give my man an ultimatum. Ultimatums do not work. I will decide what is best for me, and that's what I will do.

* If my partner can't love, respect, and appreciate me, then someone else will.

* I am NOT a victim. I AM A SURVIVOR!

* I love myself.

* I am strong.

* I am special.

* I AM A WORTHWILE PERSON!

Affirmations for the Other Woman

* I am a worthwhile person.

* I am not damaged goods.

* I am a loving, caring person.

* I do not enjoy other people's pain, nor my own.

* I have done things I regret, but so has everyone else.

* I have sinned, but so has everyone else.

* I have asked for forgiveness of my sins, so I am forgiven.

* I do not hate anyone, including the man who is using me and his partner. Hating them would only hurt me.

* I choose to forgive everyone who has hurt me—not for them, but for my own sake.

* I do not deserve to be taken for granted.

* I deserve to be respected, appreciated, and loved for who I am.

* I deserve to be the only woman in the life of the one I love.

* I do not deserve to be blamed for another person's actions.

* I assume responsibility for my own actions, and I am sorry for any pain my actions might have caused.

* I affirm that being in a relationship with a man who is committed to someone other than me is harmful to me and to all those involved.

* I affirm that ending a relationship with a man who is committed to someone other than me is painful, but it is much less painful than continuing the relationship.

* I will no longer allow myself to believe the empty promises and lies of a man who says he loves me, but continues to stay committed to someone else.

* In determining what to do with regard to my relationship with a man who is committed to another woman, I will do what is best for me—not what he wants me to do.

* After ending my relationship with this committed man, I will not allow myself to be used and treated in this manner ever again, because I deserve better.

* I affirm that a man who truly loves me would not hurt me by using me, while continuing his commitment to another woman.

* I am not a victim. I AM A SURVIVOR!

* I am strong.

* I can protect myself.

* I love myself.

* I am special.

* I AM A WORTHWHILE PERSON.

Affirmations for the Cheater

* I am a worthwhile person.

* I am not damaged goods.

* I have made mistakes that I regret, but so has everyone else.

* I have sinned, but so has everyone else.

* I have asked for forgiveness of my sins, so I am forgiven.

* I am a loving, caring person.

* I do not enjoy other people's pain.

* I assume responsibility for my own actions, and I do not blame anyone else for what I've done.

* I am sorry for the pain I have caused.

* I do not have to continue to cheat, and I affirm that I can and will resist temptations.

* I am strong.

* I am so much more than my physical body.

* I care more for myself and for my family than to continue to use my body, heart, and mind for things that cause pain to others, regardless of how much physical pleasure I might get from it.

* In ending a relationship with the other woman, I might hurt her, but continuing the relationship would be much more painful for her in the long run, so I will end it for the sake of everyone involved.

* In ending a relationship with the other woman, I know that it might cause me pain, but as I created this pain by my own bad choices, I am willing to endure the pain to make things right.

* I am not entitled to cheat.

* I will work on building my character and making life better for my partner, as well as for my children and me.

* If I determine that my relationship with my partner is unsalvageable, I will end it before becoming involved with someone else.

* I understand that by ending my relationship with my partner, I will cause pain, but that pain will heal and wouldn't hurt nearly as much as the pain caused by my infidelity.

* I am a human being who made mistakes and got on the wrong track, but I am now back on the right track.

* I am now making decisions that are positive and good for my family and me, and I deserve to be forgiven for what I've done in the past.

* I am no longer a liar.

* I am no longer a cheater.

* I love myself.

* I am special.

* I AM A WORTHWHILE PERSON!

Love Triangle DOs & DON'Ts

Because dealing with a love triangle is so painful, I've sprinkled a little humor throughout this book to lighten it up. I hope it worked. Now, I'd like to try to get another smile out of you before I close. Can I get a giggle? Okay, I'll settle for a grin, if that's all you can muster, but at least give it a shot.

DOs

* Do some 'cleaning' in the garage and have a yard sale.
There are probably a few things he's been meaning to get rid of! ~Wink~

* Wash his clothes in borax on the small load setting (less water).
A good itch might remind him of what happens when he doesn't think with his brain.

* Buy a gun and spend time practicing at the shooting range.
Make him wonder….

* Start having weekly girls' nights out, or maybe go away with friends for the weekend.
You might not hook up with anyone else, but he doesn't have to know that.

* Join a fitness center and make use of that punching bag. Picture his face on it!
That's a great stress reliever, and it would have the added bonus of getting you into better shape.

* Cook things that you love, but he hates.
Better yet, cook things he loves, fix him a plate, and add tons of salt, pepper, or sugar. Maybe some cinnamon on his steak or some cayenne in his pie!

* Wash a red shirt with his white t-shirts and socks.

* Forward his mail to Paraguay.

* Go get that new china cabinet or sofa you've been dreaming about... his treat.

* Tell him you slept with his best friend. Then tell him you didn't. Watch him squirm.

* Make a big batch of his favorite chocolate chunk cookies, and substitute Ex-lax for the chocolate.
Maybe he'll be with her when it 'hits.' Hehehe!

* Empty that bank account.
If you don't, he probably will.

* Tell him that size does count, and if his girlfriend says otherwise, she's lying.

* If you can ever pry that phone out of his hand, delete his contacts— especially the female ones.

* Make bumper stickers that read, "COPS SUCK!" and "I LOVE MARIJUANA!" and put them on his car or truck.
You can just print it out and use regular clear tape, because they'll be gone once he gets pulled over. (Don't use tape that's very sticky, because it could damage the finish.)

DON'Ts

* Do NOT cut off his penis and throw it out the window as you drive down the street.
Though it seems the perfect revenge, courts tend to frown upon that. And if you stay with him, that appendage might be useful.

* Do NOT burn the house down while he's in it.
You don't want to lose all your stuff in there. And arson is illegal.

* Do NOT poison his food or drink.
You might accidentally get poisoned yourself. And again, that whole prison thing...

* Do NOT put sugar in his gas tank.
Again, illegal.

* Do **NOT** hurt his pet!
That baby didn't hurt you and has probably treated you much better than he did!

* Do NOT drive your car into his or his girlfriend's house or apartment.
Again, illegal, and you don't want to mess up your car.

* Do NOT throw his things out of your 6th-floor apartment window.
You might hit an innocent bystander.

* Do NOT shoot his big-screen TV.
You might want to watch it. And shooting it would put holes in the wall.

* Do NOT shave off his eyebrows while he's passed out.
If you decide to let him stay, you still have to look at him, which would be creepy if his eyebrows are missing.

* Do NOT go to his office, screaming that he's a cheater who gave you herpes.
You don't want people to think you have herpes.

* Do NOT try to hold onto him just to keep her from having him.
Why cut off your nose to spite your face? Let him go! When she realizes what he's like, she'll probably kick his butt to the curb, too.

* Do NOT beat him in the head with a skillet while he's sleeping.
Again, illegal, and not worth ruining that skillet.

* Do NOT blow up his John Deere riding mower.
You could get it in the divorce.

* Do NOT tell the local drug dealer that your man is messing around with his woman.
You and that woman could get caught in the crossfire.

* Do NOT burn all his clothes.
When you watch his butt walking away after you kick him out, you don't want it to be naked.

Closing

As I've told you before, I wish I could take away your heartache and tell you how to keep him from ever cheating again. I would if I could, but I can't. All we can do is try to get through these things the best way we can and to spot it when it starts, so we don't waste so many years with a lying, cheating jerk.

Remember that you're not alone. You might not be aware of it, but you know people who have gone through the same thing. Reach out and find a support group. Some of your best allies will be women who know your pain, and maybe even his other woman. If she finds out that he's still sleeping with you, or with someone else, she'll probably feel about him the same way you do.

The best thing you can do is take care of yourself, heal, and learn from this experience. Forgiving is the best way to heal. God lets us go through these things to learn from them and to humble us. Keep in mind that what doesn't kill us makes us stronger! After going through this, you're Wonder Woman!

I wish all of you the very best of love and life. I hope you've read something in this book that gave you some hope, encouragement, and maybe even a smile. If so, please tell your suffering friends about *Cheaters & Broken Hearts*, so it can help them, too.

To anyone whose life was affected negatively by any of my behavior with men: Please forgive me. This book is my way of trying to make up for my mistakes. Take pleasure in knowing my pain.

To all my readers: YOU ARE SURVIVORS! SHOW HIM AND THE REST OF THE WORLD WHAT YOU'RE MADE OF! BE THE BEST YOU CAN BE, AND MAKE HIM AND ALL THE OTHERS WHO WERE TOO STUPID TO SEE YOUR WORTH SORRY THEY WERE SO BLIND!

NEVER FORGET YOUR AWESOMENESS!

~~~ ~~~

About the Author

Kitten is proud to be from Muscle Shoals, Alabama, which was the hit-recording capital of the world back in the 60s and 70s! Everyone wanted to record in Muscle Shoals, and many did, including Aretha Franklin, Wilson Pickett, the Rolling Stones, Bob Seger, Rod Stewart, and many, many more!

Kitten has lived most of her life in or near Muscle Shoals. She is currently in Wilmington, North Carolina with her husband. She's trying to learn to live without her little dachshund, Peej, who passed in September of 2014. Writing is Kitten's refuge and catharsis. She also enjoys movies, decorating, reading, going to the beach, and editing for other wonderful authors.

Other Books by Kitten K. Jackson

Keeping Secrets
Fiction

Sparks fly when Greg returns to Pensacola to be with Abbie. When she realizes who he is, she must decide whether to take a chance with the now attractive and charming man who forcefully took her years ago, or to trust her instincts... and the police. Has he changed, or is he guilty of a double murder? Abbie's heart says, "Go for it," but her gut screams, "Run!"

A tormented man, Greg Parker, is obsessed with a woman he forcefully took against her will 16 years ago, but hasn't seen since then. Over the years, he transforms himself from Johnny Moretti, the skinny geek, into a very attractive and manipulative man, not even recognizable to himself.

The woman, Abbie Kolbeck, is haunted by the memory of Johnny—someone she trusted. When he contacts her after all those years, she is passionately drawn to him, believing the familiar feeling between them means their union is fate. She has no idea she's falling for the man who hurt her so long ago.

After a whirlwind romance, Abbie finds that Greg is being investigated for the murder of his best friend and the friend's girlfriend. And after a not-so-gentle session in bed, she realizes that he's the man she forgave for raping her.

Abbie desperately wants to believe Greg's denials, but she's torn between her feelings for him and her desire to protect her daughter and herself from a man the police are telling her is a murderer.

Keeping Secrets II: No More Skeletons
Fiction

That's right—Greg is back! Abbie hopes her promise not to tell the police about the murders, as long as Greg stays away, will keep her and her family safe. But not even his fear of going to prison for murder could keep Greg away from Abbie. This time, however, it's not just Abbie that he wants. He's determined to make sure Taylor knows their secret.

After a visit with Ellen, who allowed him to be brutalized as a child, Greg comes undone. His obsession drives him to abduct Abbie and Taylor, taking them on a five-state crime spree, desperate to flee from multiple law enforcement agencies.

As Abbie struggles with her convictions, her emotions, and her overwhelming need to protect Taylor, the body count rises.

What will Abbie do when the opportunity to escape presents itself? And what will Greg do when faced with the choice of saving Abbie's life, or his own?

Keeping Secrets III: Generational Curses
Fiction
To be published in Summer of 2015.

Reviews are greatly appreciated!
Thank you!